W9-AHL-968

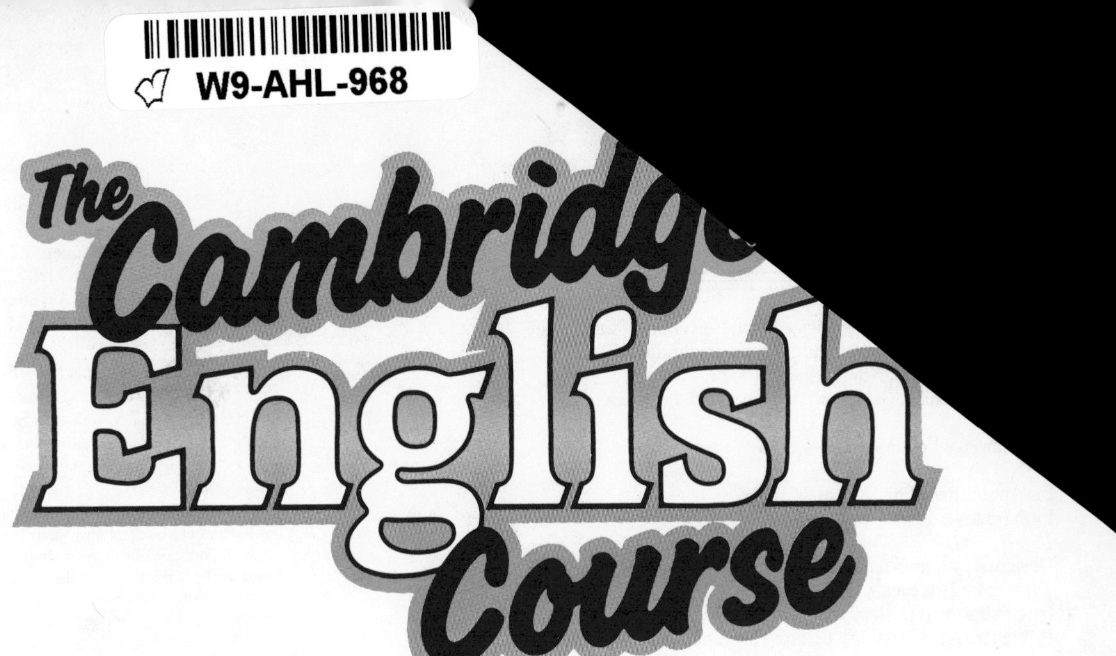

Michael Swan and Catherine Walter

Cambridge University Press
Cambridge London New York New Rochelle Melbourne Sydney

...yndicate of the University of Cambridge
...umpington Street, Cambridge CB2 1RP
...et, New York, NY 10022, USA
...Road, Oakleigh, Melbourne 3166, Australia

...nbridge University Press 1985

First published 1985
Fifth printing 1986

Designed by John Youé and Associates, Croydon, Surrey
Typeset by Text Filmsetters Limited, London
Origination by BTA Reprographics Limited, London
Printed in Great Britain by Blantyre Printing and Binding, Glasgow

ISBN 0 521 28983 2 Practice Book 2

ISBN 0 521 28984 X Student's Book 2
Split edition: ISBN 0 521 33757 7 Part A
ISBN 0 521 33758 5 Part B
ISBN 0 521 33759 3 Part C

ISBN 0 521 28982 3 Teacher's Book 2
ISBN 0 521 31626 X Test Book 2
ISBN 0 521 24817 5 Cassette Set 2
ISBN 0 521 30324 9 Student's Cassette 2

Copyright
The law allows a reader to make a single copy of part of a book for purposes of private study. It does not allow the copying of entire books or the making of multiple copies of extracts. Written permission for any such copying must always be obtained from the publisher in advance.

Acknowledgements

The authors and publishers are grateful to the following copyright owners for permission to reproduce photographs, illustrations and texts.
Every endeavour has been made to contact copyright owners and apologies are expressed for any omissions.

page 4: Jon Miller. page 7: Reproduced by permission of the *Deutsches Archäologisches Institut*, Rome. page 9: Bob Harvey. page 10: Kate Simunek. page 11: *Time* Inc., New York; *br* Kate Simunek. page 13: *t* and *b* Reproduced by permission of *Punch*. page 14: *bl* Reproduced by permission of *Punch*; *br* © Hamlyn Publishing Group Ltd. page 20: Tony Streek. page 22: *c* from the *Oxford Mail*. page 23: *br* Reproduced by permission of *Punch*. page 24: Harmsworth Publishers Ltd. page 26: *bl* Guinness Superlatives Ltd; *tr* Harmsworth Publishers Ltd; *br* Harmsworth Publishers Ltd. page 29: Val Sangster. page 30: *tl* from *Enquiry* by Dick Francis, Pan Books Ltd; *tr* Photograph, Clive Totman; *bl* Odette Buchanan. page 31: Bob Harvey. page 34: *t* Reproduced by permission of the Controller of Her Majesty's Stationery Office; *b* Reproduced by permission of *Punch*. page 36: Text, Based on an extract from *London: Your Sightseeing Guide*, published by the British Tourist Authority in 1972; Map, Malcolm Ward. page 40: Leaflets published by the GLC. page 42: Reproduced by permission of *Punch*. page 45: *tr* by John Hill of *The Sun*, quoted from *Cross Your Fingers, Spit in Your Hat* by Alvin Schwartz, published by Andre Deutsch, 1976; *b* from the *Longman Active Study Dictionary of English* edited by Della Summers, Longman, 1983. page 46: Reproduced by permission of *Punch*. page 48: Odette Buchanan. page 50: Reproduced by permission of *Punch*. page 51: Malcolm Ward. page 52: *t* and *b* Kate Simunek. page 55: Malcolm Ward. page 58: 'I Like That Stuff' from *Poems* by Adrian Mitchell, published by Jonathan Cape Ltd. page 61: Alexa Rutherford. page 64: from *Children's Letters to God* by Marshall and Hample, published by Fontana. page 66: A and D Reproduced by permission of *Punch*; B from *Laughter Cartoons*, Syndication International; C Harmsworth Publishers Ltd; E © McMurphy, from Hamlyn Publishing Group. page 68: from *The Observer*, 29/7/84. page 70: Reproduced by permission of *Punch*. page 71: Article reproduced from *Punch*; *cr* Harmsworth Publishers Ltd; *br* © Mirror Books, Syndication International. page 76: Harmsworth Publishers Ltd. page 77: *t* © The Collection Hamish Hamilton 1963, from *Vintage Thurber* edited by Helen Thurber, published by Hamish Hamilton, Copyright © 1940 James Thurber, © 1968 Helen Thurber, from *Fables For Our Time*, published by Harper & Row; *b* from the *Sunday Express*. page 80: *l* from Isaac Asimov's *Book of Facts*, copyright © 1979 by Red Dembner Enterprises Corp; *r* Odette Buchanan. page 82: from *Curious Facts* by John May. page 85: Harmsworth Publishers Ltd. page 86: *t* Bob Harvey; *b* Reprinted from *Letters from a Fainthearted Feminist* by Jill Tweedie, first published in Great Britain by Robson Books Ltd, 1982. page 92: *t* Copyright © The Diagram Group, adapted from *How to Hold a Crocodile*, with permission; *b* Bob Harvey. page 94: Odette Buchanan. page 95: Dr M. McCarthy. page 96: Reproduced by permission of *Punch*. page 97: *t* and *bl* Reproduced by permission of *Punch*; *br* from Isaac Asimov's *Book of Facts*, copyright © 1979 by Red Dembner Enterprises Corp. page 98: Reproduced with permission from the leaflet *How To Put Things Right*, published by the Office of Fair Trading. page 101: *l* and *r* Harmsworth Publishers Ltd. page 105: *tl* © 1939 Chappell & Co Inc., New York, reproduced by permission of Chappell Music Ltd and International Music Publications; *tr* Reproduced by permission of *Punch*; *bl* Harmsworth Publishers Ltd. page 106: Harmsworth Publishers Ltd. page 107: Reproduced by permission of *Punch*. page 109: Roadsigns from the *Highway Code*, published by Her Majesty's Stationery Office, reproduced with permission of the publisher; *r* © 1981 *New Statesman*, reprinted with permission. page 111: *tr* Guinness Superlatives Ltd; *cr* The Sunday Times; *br* © 1981 Washington Post Writers Group, reprinted by permission. page 114: Val Sangster. page 116: Mitchell Beazley Encyclopaedias Ltd, London. page 119: Malcolm Ward. page 120: Reproduced with permission of *Punch*. page 121: Malcolm Ward. page 126: Malcolm Ward. page 127: by permission of Cosmopolitan UK. page 131: *c* and *br* Reproduced by permission of *Punch*. page 132: *tl Selected Poems* translation Ian Milner and George Theiner (Penguin Modern European Poets, 1967), © Miroslav Holub 1967, translation copyright © Penguin Books Ltd 1967; *tr* From the 1968 *Daily Mirror* Children's Literary Competition. page 133: *tl* © Guinness Superlatives Ltd; *br* Odette Buchanan. page 134: Odette Buchanan. page 135: Adapted from *People's Weekly; bl* Bob Harvey. page 141: *r* From *Car Driving in Two Weeks*, published by Paperfronts, Elliot Right Way Books, Kingswood, Surrey.

(*t* = top *b* = bottom *c* = centre *r* = right *l* = left)

Contents

Acknowledgements 2
Unit 1 People 4
Unit 2 Other worlds 8
Unit 3 The past 14
Unit 4 Comparisons 18
Unit 5 Asking and offering 22
Unit 6 The future 25
Unit 7 Things that have happened 28
Unit 8 Know before you go 34
Unit 9 Problems 38
Unit 10 If and when 43
Unit 12 Causes and origins 50
Unit 13 Descriptions 55
Unit 14 Families 60
Unit 15 Hopes and wishes 64
Unit 16 Money 70
Unit 17 Before and after 74
Unit 18 Facts and opinions 79
Unit 19 Small talk 84
Unit 20 Do it 89
Unit 21 Technology 95
Unit 23 Feelings 101
Unit 24 Authority 106
Unit 25 Look and listen 110
Unit 26 Different kinds 114
Unit 27 Changes 119
Unit 28 Health 125
Unit 29 Heads 130
Unit 30 Work 134
Unit 31 Travel 139
Answers to Exercises 142

Unit 1 People

A Tell me about yourself

1 Fill in the gaps in the conversations.

TOM: Jake, ... like to .... my friend Alice.
ALICE: How ....?
JAKE: How ....?

———

ANN: Andy, ... is Louise.
ANDY: Hello, Louise. I'm .... to .... you.

———

JOE: Hello, Phil. How ....?
PHIL: Fine, ..., Joe. .... to see you again.

———

CATHY: Janet, ... Susan?
JANET: No. How do you do? I've heard .... much .... you.

———

JUDY: .... I introduce ....?
My .... Judy Gower.
RUTH: Hello. I'm Ruth Collins. I'm sorry, I didn't .... your name.

———

KATE: Where are you from?
MARK: Canada.
KATE: .... in Canada?
MARK: Toronto.

———

STEVE: .... me. .... you Liz Bush?
LIZ: Yes, that's ....

2 Make questions to find out the following information. Be careful of the word order.

1. The address of the girl with red hair.
Where does the girl with red hair live?
(NOT ~~*Where lives...*~~)
2. The place where John's sister works.
Where .... John's sister ....
3. The month when Sally usually goes on holiday.
When ....
4. The languages that Mr Campbell speaks.
What languages ....
5. The price of a tube of toothpaste.
How much ....
6. The departure time of the next train.
What time .... leave?
7. The boss's way of spending his weekends.
How ....

3 Make some 'follow-up' questions.

1. My brother Pat usually gets up at five o'clock.
   Does *he get up at five o'clock on Sundays?*
   Does *he go to work early?*
   Why *does he get up so early?*
2. George plays the piano.
   How well ....
   How often ....
   Where ....
   .... enjoy playing the piano?
3. Susan's parents often go to Spain.
   How often ....
   Do .... summer?
   What part of Spain .... go to?
   Do ....
   Portugal?
4. Edna sells some lovely pictures.
   What kind of pictures ....
   .... other things?
5. My boss smokes 50 cigarettes a day.
   Why ....
   .... in the office?
6. I speak four languages.
   What ....
   ....
   How well ....
   ....
7. Anne goes to evening classes.
   Why ....
   How often ....

4 Write sentences with *not*.

1. My brother speaks French. (German)
   He does not speak German.
2. Tobacconists sell cigarettes. (stamps)
   ....
3. She works from Monday to Friday. (on Saturdays)
   ....
4. Harry plays the trumpet and saxophone. (piano)
   ....
5. Her parents want her to marry an American. (an Englishman)
   ....
6. That car belongs to me. (my father)
   ....
7. I like skiing. (swimming)
   ....
8. He reads newspapers. (books)
   ....
9. She works with children. (old people)
   ....

5 **Can you complete the table?**

FIRST PERSON	THIRD PERSON
I work	he/she works
I live	he/she ....
I think	he/she ....
I enjoy	he/she ....
I watch	he/she watches
I wish	he/she ....
I dress	he/she ....
I try	he/she tries
I fly	he/she ....
I reply	he/she ....

Now can you give the third person singular (*he/she/it...*) of these verbs?

start ....
catch ....
cry ....
push ....
stop ....
hope ....
give ....
stand ....
press ....
dry ....
play ....
crash ....

B Married with two children

1 **Frequency adverbs. Look at these sentences from the interviews (Student's Book Exercise 3).**

'Do you drink?' ***'Occasionally.'***
'Do you go to church?' ***'Not very often.'***
I ***very rarely*** *read a newspaper.*

Now can you put these adverbs in order of frequency, from most often to least often?

hardly ever	never	occasionally	often
quite often	rarely	sometimes	very often

1. very often
2. ....
3. ....
4. ....
5. ....
6. ....
7. ....
8. never

Now say how often you do these things.

1. I .... smoke.
2. I .... talk to myself.
3. I .... read thrillers.
4. I .... write letters.
5. I .... travel by air.
6. I .... fall in love.
7. I .... have bad dreams.
8. I .... get headaches.
9. I .... lose my temper.
10. I .... forget people's names.
11. I .... tell the truth.
12. I .... go swimming.

2 **Have you got these things? Write ten or more sentences. Begin *I've got…* or *I haven't got…* Examples:**

I've got a cat.

I haven't got a bicycle.

a cat a dog a guitar a piano
a French dictionary a camera a bicycle
a pink shirt a typewriter a handbag
a pair of brown shoes a garden a calculator
blue eyes

3 **Put the right words with the different parts of the body.**

arm beard chest ear eye face finger foot hair hand head knee leg mouth neck nose shoulder stomach

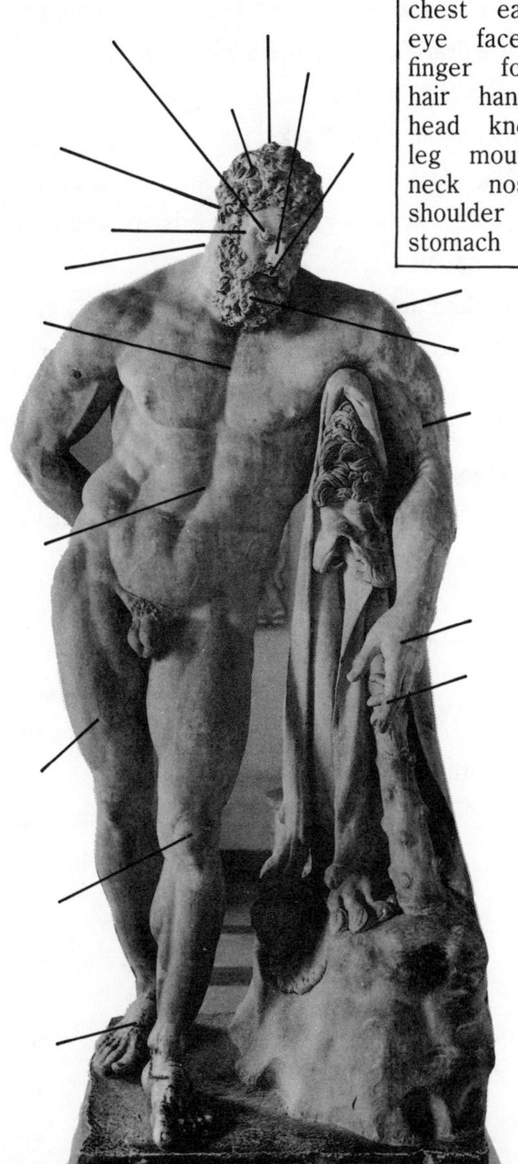

4 **Complete the text with the words and expressions from the box.**

always beautiful blue each other forget girlfriend her is doing laughed listen to long fair neither…nor nose person quite Shakespeare's smile tired worked

My first real .... was a very .... girl called Penny. She was .... tall, ... slim .... fat, with a lovely figure. She had .... hair and .... eyes, a funny short ...., and a wide mouth with a wonderful ...., like the sun coming out. Her voice was soft and nice to .... She had a great sense of humour, and we .... a lot. At nights she .... as a nurse in a mental hospital, and she was often very .... when we saw ...., but she was .... fun to be with. She was a very talented actress, and I will never .... her playing Hermione in a student production of .... *Winter's Tale.* Penny was a lovely ...., and I was lucky to know .... I often wonder what she .... now.

5 **Write a description of yourself, or of somebody you like. Use some words and expressions from Exercise 4.**

I'm tall and fair, with blue eyes and a small nose. My feet are quite big, but I think I'm quite nice-looking. I like dancing and listening to music.

Unit 2

Other worlds

A There's a strange light in the sky

1 **Fill in the gaps with words and expressions from the box.**

all right	blouse	brown	dress	experience	hat	inside	know	light	pattern
shirt	since	skirt	suit	visitor	what	laughing	making	saying	shouting
is answering	is just arriving	is getting out	is introducing	is looking	is talking				
are coming down	are shaking	she's asking	he's wearing	she's wearing					

– and Mrs Rask's car .... in front of the palace. This is a historic moment – as I am sure you ...., she is the first Fantasian president to visit our country .... 1954. President and Mrs Martin .... the steps to welcome her. And now the car has stopped, and Mrs Rask .... There seems to be some problem with the door. No, it's .... President Martin and Mrs Rask .... hands – and the crowds are going wild – people are cheering and .... What an .... this is! And now Mrs Martin .... to the Fantasian president. I expect .... if she had a good journey. The Fantasian president .... Mrs Martin – I don't know what she's .... but she's obviously .... a joke – everybody's .... Now President Martin .... the Foreign Minister and his staff to our distinguished .... I must say that Mrs Rask .... *beautiful* – .... Fantasian national costume: a long green and gold silk .... with a lovely .... of flowers, and a tall red .... President and Mrs Martin are dressed very simply, as usual: .... a dark blue .... with a .... blue .... and black tie, and Mrs Martin is wearing a brown tweed .... with a white .... and light .... shoes. .... an experience this is! What a historic moment! And now they're going .... the palace. The President is leading the way –

2 Write the *-ing* forms.

talk ......talking......
answer ....
ask ....
look ....
say ....

arrive ......arriving......
introduce ....
come ....
shake ....

get ......getting......
stop ....
sit ....
run ....

lie ......lying......
die ....

work ....
make ....
hit ....
live ....
slim ....
hear ....

3 Here are pieces of some pictures. What do you think the woman is doing in each one?

A She is drinking a glass of wine.
B She is...

C ....
D ....

E ....
F ....

G ....
H ....

I ....
J ....

(Answers on page 142.)

4 Do you know the names of all these articles of clothing? Use your dictionary to help you.

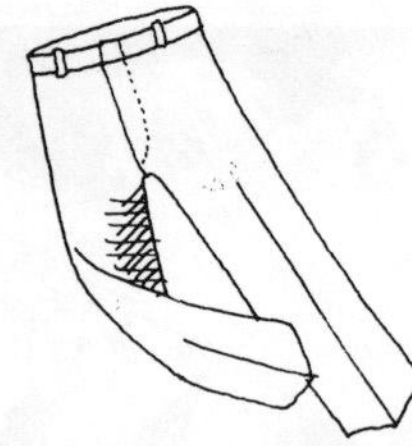

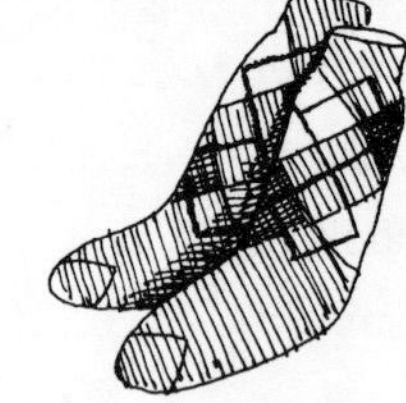

....

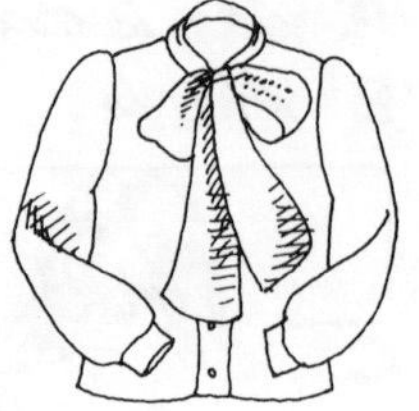

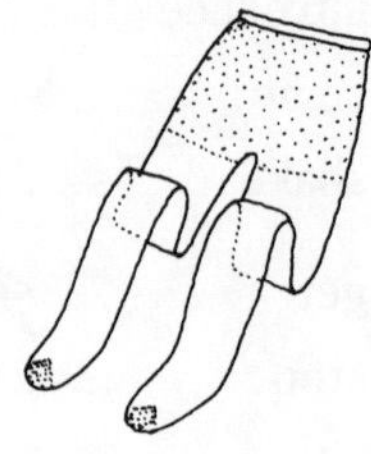

....

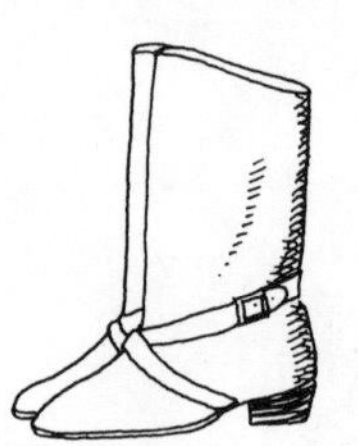
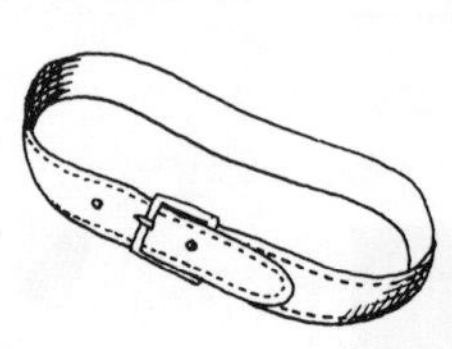
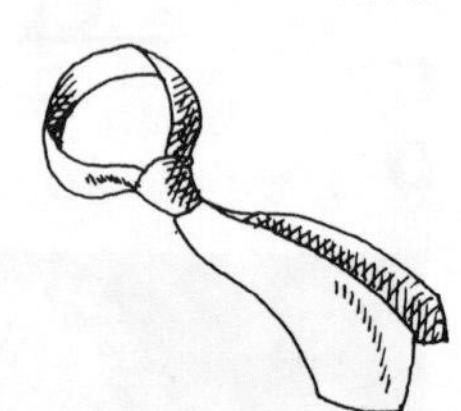
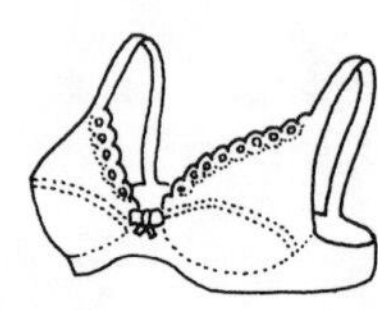
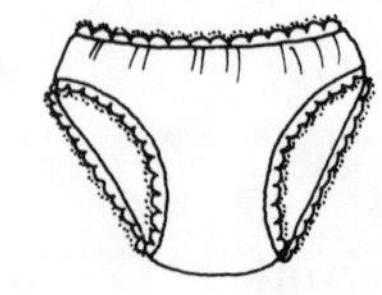

....

....

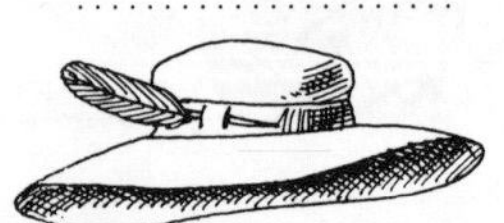

....

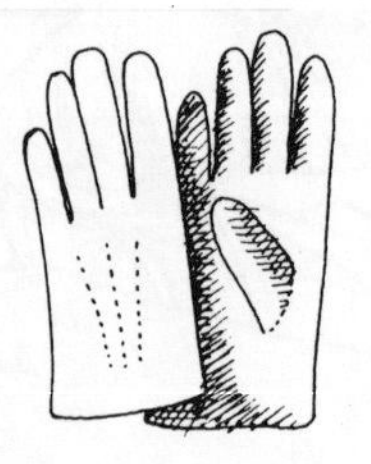

....

5 Make questions. Be careful of the word order.

1. Where|the President and his wife|standing?
   Where are the President and his wife standing?
   (NOT ~~*Where are standing*~~ ...)
2. What|Mrs Andrews|writing?
   ....
3. What|that girl|eating?
   ....
4. Why|those old men|singing?
   ....
5. Why|the car|making a funny noise?
   ....
6. What|Mrs Harris|trying to say?
   ....
7. Where|your aunt|working just now?
   ....
8. Dr Parker|working|today?
   ....
9. your TV|working all right?
   ....

6 Read the text. You can use a dictionary if you want to. Then decide which picture shows the woman's dream.

She glanced about swiftly, as if expecting someone there before her. She seemed disappointed; the space between the pillars was empty.

Her husband appeared in a triangular door. "Did you call?" he asked irritably.

"No!"

"I thought I heard you cry out."

"Did I? I was almost asleep and had a dream!"

"In the daytime? You don't often do that."

She sat as if struck in the face by the dream. "How strange, how very strange," she murmured. "The dream."

"Oh?" He evidently wished to return to his book.

"I dreamed about a man."

"A man?"

"A tall man, six feet one inch tall."

"How absurd; a giant, a misshapen giant."

"Somehow"– she tried the words – "he looked all right. In spite of being tall. And he had – oh, I know you'll think it silly – he had *blue* eyes!"

"Blue eyes! Gods!" cried Mr K. "What'll you dream next? I suppose he had *black* hair?"

"How did you *guess*?" She was excited.

"I picked the most unlikely color," he replied coldly.

"Well, black it was!" she cried. "And he had a very white skin; oh, he was *most* unusual! He was dressed in a strange uniform and he came down out of the sky and spoke pleasantly to me." She smiled.

"Out of the sky; what nonsense!"

"He came in a metal thing that glittered in the sun," she remembered. She closed her eyes to shape it again. "I dreamed there was the sky and something sparkled like a coin thrown into the air, and suddenly it grew large and fell down softly to land, a long silver craft, round and alien. And a door opened in the side of the silver object and this tall man stepped out."

"If you worked harder you wouldn't have these silly dreams."

"I rather enjoyed it," she replied, lying back. "I never suspected myself of such an imagination. Black hair, blue eyes, and white skin! What a strange man, and yet – quite handsome."

"Wishful thinking."

"You're unkind. I didn't think him up on purpose; he just came in my mind while I drowsed. It wasn't like a dream. It was so unexpected and different. He looked at me and he said, 'I've come from the third planet in my ship. My name is Nathaniel York –'"

"A stupid name; it's no name at all," objected the husband.

"Of course it's stupid, because it's a dream," she explained softly. "And he said, 'This is the first trip across space. There are only two of us in our ship, myself and my friend Bert.'"

"*Another* stupid name."

"And he said, 'We're from a city on *Earth*; that's the name of our planet,'" continued Mrs K. "That's what he said. 'Earth' was the name he spoke. And he used another language. Somehow I understood him. With my mind. Telepathy, I suppose."

Mr K turned away. She stopped him with a word. "Yll?" she called quietly. "Do you ever wonder if – well, if there *are* people living on the third planet?"

"The third planet is incapable of supporting life," stated the husband patiently. "Our scientists have said there's far too much oxygen in their atmosphere."

"But wouldn't it be fascinating if there *were* people? And they traveled through space in some sort of ship?"

(from *The Martian Chronicles* by Ray Bradbury)

A

B

C

B What do you believe in?

1 Add one of these to each sentence.

always	at the moment	never	often	right now	this week	today	usually

1. You're looking very beautiful.

 ....

2. He's talking on another line.

 ....

3. I play tennis on Wednesdays.

 ....

4. Gloria goes to foreign films.

 ....

5. He buys his clothes in Oxford.

 ....

6. My cousin is staying at our house.

 ....

7. Mary is shopping; she'll be back in about half an hour.

 ....

 ....

8. I see Joe at the swimming pool.

 ....

2 Put one or more suitable words in each blank. You can use your imagination.

1. Sarah .... to the cinema every weekend.
2. What .... at?
3. John can't come to the phone right now – .... a bath.
4. I usually .... coffee for breakfast.
5. Food prices .... very fast at the moment.
6. My friend Stan .... at ten o'clock on Saturdays.
7. Look – somebody .... you.
8. Excuse me – .... my foot.
9. Mary .... very hard these days.
10. What languages ....?

3 Say these words with the correct stress.

reason **non**sense **rub**bish
definitely **in**terest **tra**vel
cheerful **vi**sitor

be**lief** ma**chine** ex**plain**
expe**ri**ence ex**pres**sion

intro**duce** under**stand** natio**na**lity

"May I say how much I admire the care you take with your appearance? So many dead women just let themselves go."

"I bet you didn't believe in him, either!"

4 Fill in the blanks with words and expressions from the box.

also certainly either in little may or other probably so somewhere that yet

I am not at all a religious person, and I do not believe in God, reincarnation, ghosts .... life after death.
On the other hand, I think that we probably understand very .... about the universe, and that there are many things that we cannot explain .... For example, some of the stories about UFOs .... be true. We are .... not the only intelligent beings in the universe, ... perhaps there are other people .... who are trying to make contact with us.
I believe .... telepathy, and I .... think that the human mind may have other powers that we do not understand. But I .... do not believe .... we can predict the future, ... by horoscopes or by any .... method.

5 Now write about your beliefs. Try to use the expressions in the box.

Unit 3

The past

A A true story

1 Read the text and fill in the gaps with words from the two lists.

There have been many reports of 'UFOs' (unidentified flying objects) over the last few years. Many people believe that these UFOs come from other worlds, far away in space. Here is one report from an American newspaper.

LIST 1
Put the past tenses of these verbs into the gaps marked '1'.
come come feel
have leave make
phone run see see
say speak stay stop

LIST 2
Put these words into the gaps marked '2'.
and and and but
that then when
when who

On June 14th, in Carmel, Indiana, a woman 1 .... a large strange bright light moving around in the sky. The woman, Mrs Dora Gabb, 34, 1 .... the police 2 ....
1 .... to Patrolman Conrad Brown, 2 ....
1 .... straight to her house to investigate. 2 .... he arrived there was nothing to be seen, 2 .... ten minutes later Mrs Gabb's 14-year-old daughter Leslie 1 .... into the house screaming. Leslie 1 .... 2 .... she and a girlfriend were riding on motor-bicycles in the woods 2 .... they
1 .... 'a large object, bigger than a house' directly in front of them, low in the sky. It 1 .... a green top, white sides, a reddish purple tail, and lights of purple, green, gold, red and blue. It
1 .... no sound. The girls' bicycles 1 ....
working, 2 .... the girls '1 .... strange'. The spaceship 1 .... down lower, 2 ....
1 .... for some time about 100 feet above the ground, not moving. 2 ...., with a whistling sound, it 1 ....
at high speed.

'I knew she was going out with a coloured chap, but never thought it was green.'

"... and the next contestant hoping to become Miss Universe..."

2 This is part of a conversation between a policeman and a young woman. Fill in the gaps. The words in the box will help you.

arrive do go make see stop take telephone travel watch

POLICEMAN: What time .... work yesterday?

WOMAN: I don't know. About half past five.

POL: And where .... after that?

WOM: I went straight home.

POL: I see. How .... home? By bus?

WOM: Yes.

POL: What bus ....?

WOM: I don't remember.

POL: All right. What time .... home?

WOM: Oh, around six, I suppose.

POL: .... anybody you knew on the way?

WOM: I don't think so. I don't remember.

POL: What .... when you got home?

WOM: Made a cup of tea and put the TV on.

POL: Oh, yes. What programme ....?

WOM: 'Front page'.

POL: 'Front page' wasn't on last night.

WOM: I've got it recorded on video.

POL: I see. .... any phone calls?

WOM: Pardon?

POL: .... anybody?

WOM: I might have done. I don't remember.

3 Write sentences with *not*.

1. Beethoven wrote symphonies. (books)
   Beethoven did not write books.
2. I went to the seaside last year. (the mountains)
   ....
   ....
3. I found the shoes I wanted. (the sweater)
   ....
   ....
4. My mother lived abroad when she was young. (in Britain)
   ....
   ....
5. She fell in love with an American. (an Englishman)
   ....
   ....
6. Her parents wanted her to marry an Englishman. (the American)
   Her parents did not want her to marry the American.
7. She did what she wanted. (what her parents wanted)
   ....
   ....
8. It snowed yesterday. (rain)
   ....

4 **Write down five things that you did not do yesterday. Write your answer on a separate sheet of paper.**

5 **Complete the table.**

INFINITIVE	PAST TENSE	INFINITIVE	PAST TENSE	INFINITIVE	PAST TENSE
work	worked	stop	....	hope	....
start	....	shop	....	like	....
play	....	drop	....	hate	....
watch	....	fit	....		
fill	....	prefer	....		

B Did you have a good day?

1 **Read the dialogue (Student's Book Exercise 1, page 16) again. Then complete the following conversation.**

ANN: Hello, darling. .... a nice day?

PAT: So-so. John came in this morning, and said he .... to talk to me.

ANN: What ....?

PAT: Oh, his marriage, as .... We .... lunch together, and we had a long ...., and he said he felt better.

ANN: Where .... have lunch? Somewhere ....?

PAT: No, we went to the pub round the .... I just had a beer and a sandwich. Then in the afternoon Alice phoned and talked .... hours. Just .... I was trying to do some ....

ANN: I *am* sorry. It .... like a difficult day.

PAT: Well, it was quite interesting, but I .... get much work done.

2 **Put in the right tense (simple past or past progressive).**

1. When I .... the house, I .... some old letters. (*clean*; *find*)
2. The doorbell .... while I .... a bath. (*ring*; *have*)
3. We .... an accident when we .... back from holiday. (*have*; *come*)
4. When I looked out of the window, I .... that it .... (*realise*; *rain*)
5. I .... my wife when we .... in Washington. (*meet*; *live*)
6. I .... at a garage because the car .... badly. (*stop*; *run*)
7. I suddenly .... of you while I .... (*think*; *wash up*)
8. She .... to sleep while I .... her about my holidays. (*go*; *tell*)
9. When I .... up, water .... through the ceiling. (*look*; *come*)

3 Revision. Put in the right prepositions. (Sometimes no preposition is necessary.)

1. I'm going away tomorrow. I'll see you again .... three weeks.
2. She works .... nine .... five except .... Saturdays.
3. I was born .... the first day of spring.
4. Can you come and stay with us .... August?
5. What are you doing .... this evening?
6. I'm working until seven, but I'm free .... that.
7. We're going to Morocco in May .... three weeks.
8. Let's go walking .... the weekend.
9. Are you free .... next Monday?
10. I'll see you .... eight o'clock.
11. Telephone me .... six, or it will be too late.
12. I always work better .... the morning than .... the afternoon.

4 Try the crossword.

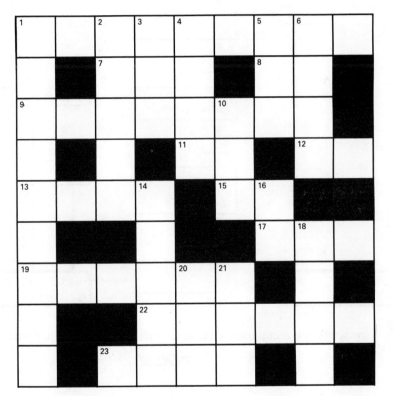

1		2	3	4		5	6	
		7				8		
9					10			
				11			12	
13			14		15	16		
						17	18	
19				20	21			
			22					
		23						

ACROSS

1. Not easy.
7. Go fast on foot.
8. I was tired, ... I went to bed.
9. A number between twelve and twenty.
11. Are you free .... Monday evening?
12. Let's .... to Scotland for our holiday.
13. He's fat because he .... too much.
15. 'What do you ....?' 'I'm a musician.'
17. Travel by air.
19. .... me. Have you got a light?
22. '........... very much.' 'Not at all.'
23. Person who uses.

DOWN

1. Not similar.
2. Oranges, bananas, apples, lemons.
3. Some coats are made from it.
4. The opposite of *out of*.
5. You .... a knife for cutting things.
6. Sorry I'm late. Have you been waiting ....?
10. Not the beginning; not the middle.
14. The opposite of *opens*.
16. Could I have a glass .... water?
18. Would you .... something to eat?
20. 'Why isn't Alice here?' '........... isn't feeling very well.'
21. You hear with it.

(Solution on page 142.)

Unit 4

Comparisons

Things are different

1 **Look at the diagram, and study the rules for making comparative and superlative adjectives.**

HOW TO MAKE COMPARATIVE AND SUPERLATIVE ADJECTIVES

START HERE. → Has the adjective got one syllable? → No. → Has the adjective got two syllables? → No. → PUT *MORE/MOST* BEFORE THE ADJECTIVE.

Has the adjective got one syllable? → Yes. → Does the adjective end in *-e*? → Yes. → ADD *-R/-ST* TO THE ADJECTIVE.

Does the adjective end in *-e*? → No. → Has the adjective got two vowels? → Yes. → ADD *-ER/-EST* TO THE ADJECTIVE.

Has the adjective got two vowels? → No. → Does the adjective end in two consonants? → Yes. → ADD *-ER/-EST* TO THE ADJECTIVE.

Does the adjective end in two consonants? → No. → Double the last letter. → ADD *-ER/-EST* TO THE ADJECTIVE.

Has the adjective got two syllables? → Yes. → Does the adjective end in *-y*? → No. → PUT *MORE/MOST* BEFORE THE ADJECTIVE.

Does the adjective end in *-y*? → Yes. → Change to *y* to *i*. → ADD *-ER/-EST* TO THE ADJECTIVE.

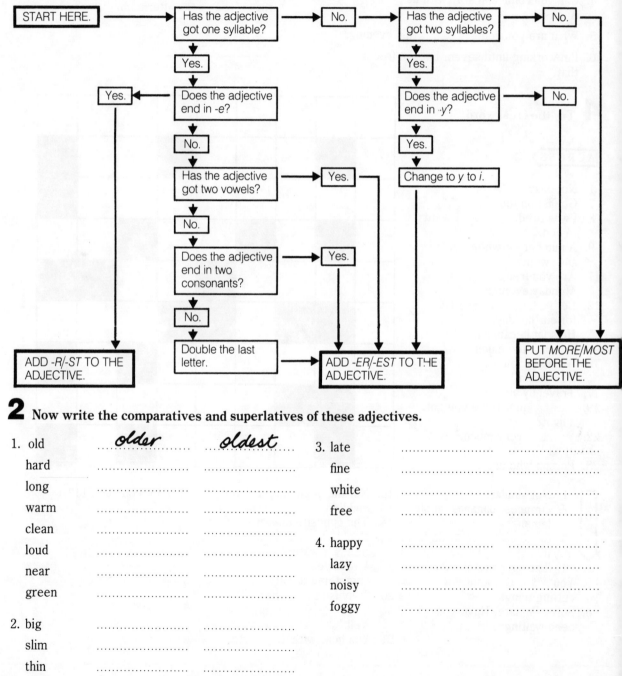

2 **Now write the comparatives and superlatives of these adjectives.**

1. old ......older...... ......oldest......
   hard ....
   long ....
   warm ....
   clean ....
   loud ....
   near ....
   green ....

2. big ....
   slim ....
   thin ....

3. late ....
   fine ....
   white ....
   free ....

4. happy ....
   lazy ....
   noisy ....
   foggy ....

5. boring ....
cheerful ....
expensive ....

6. fat ....
pure ....
cool ....
sorry ....
red ....
large ....
useful ....
close ....
light ....
fit ....

3 Put in *as* or *than*.

1. A diamond is harder .... iron.
2. Wales is not as big .... Scotland.
3. I work in the same office .... my brother.
4. On average, women live longer .... men.
5. Cheese has more calories .... bread.
6. England is not nearly as big .... New Zealand.
7. She plays much better .... I do.
8. Your eyes are almost the same colour .... mine.
9. I think football is more interesting .... tennis.
10. Eat .... much .... you like.

4 Write two sentences to compare each of the following.

1. a mouse and a cat
A mouse is smaller than a cat.
A cat can run faster than a mouse.
2. Britain and your country
....
....
3. the United States and the USSR
....
....
4. a car and a bicycle
....
....
5. men and women
....
....
6. yourself and another person
....
....

5 **Look at the two pictures. They are not quite the same. For example, in picture B the man's hair is longer. Can you find ten more differences? (The solution is on page 142.)**

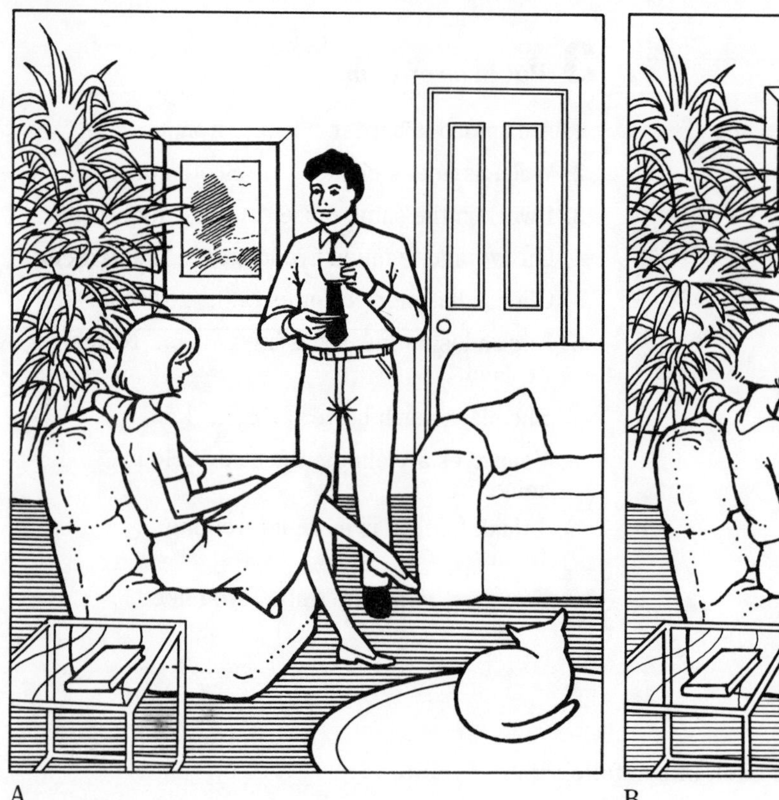

A

B

6 **Choose the correct words to complete the sentences.**

1. Your English is much *better / best* than mine.
2. The *better / best* whisky comes from Scotland.
3. We've had much *more / most* rain this year than last year.
4. The place that gets the *more / most* rain in the world is a mountain in Hawaii.
5. In a 'slow bicycle race', the winner is the person who goes the *less / least* distance in three minutes.
6. I don't know much, but she knows even *less / least* than I do.
7. Which month has the *fewer / fewest* days?
8. There are *fewer / fewest* Jews in Israel than in New York.
9. 'Are you any good at tennis?' 'I'm the *worse / worst* tennis-player in the world.'
10. 'How's your headache?' 'It's getting *worse / worst.*'
11. I'll get you an aspirin. That'll make you feel *better / best.*
12. People say that Rolls Royce make the *better / best* cars in the world.

7 **Strange but true. Read this with a dictionary.**

The population of Mexico City is twice as big as the population of Norway.

Tortoises live longer than people; some bacteria live longer than tortoises. Some trees live for over 3,000 years.

In the 18th century a Russian woman had 69 children.

The world record for water-skiing is faster than the world record for Alpine skiing.

The Olympic weightlifting champion Paul Anderson lifted 6,270 pounds (2,850 kilos) in 1957, in a 'backlift'. This is as heavy as three football teams plus five more men.

The nucleus of a hydrogen atom, multiplied 100,000 million times, would be as big as this dot: •

B People are different

1 Study the examples, and then decide where to put *both* in each sentence.

ONE-WORD VERBS
We **both speak** Chinese.
My sister and I **both like** music.

TWO-WORD VERBS
We **were both born** in September.
They **have both studied** in the USA.
Anne and Peter **can both sing** very well.

AM/ARE/WAS/WERE
We **are both** fair-haired.
The two children **were both** very hungry.

1. My parents ^ work in the same bank.
2. When I arrived, they were cooking.
3. You look like your mother.
4. Our children are tall and slim.
5. We have been in hospital recently.
6. The cars cost a fortune.
7. Alice and Judy can play chess.
8. I think those trees are going to die.

2 Fill in the gaps with words from the box.

as as as much as better both both of them from he him like more more much than than that that which

Helen could not decide .... of the boys she liked best. .... were old friends of hers, and they .... had nice personalities. Rob was quite similar to her. He had the same interests .... her, and they enjoyed doing things together. She was a bit older ...., but that was not very important. He was very grown-up and mature, and much .... self-confident .... John. She was very fond of him and she knew .... he loved her. Only she was not sure .... he loved her .... John. John was very different .... her – he was not really .... anybody else she had ever met – and that made him .... interesting, in a way. He had travelled .... more than her, and .... could talk for hours about places that she had never seen, He was .... -looking than Rob, too – taller and stronger. And his eyes were the same colour .... the sea on a summer day. But John was strange. She never quite knew what he was thinking, and he sometimes did unexpected things that worried her.

3 Now continue the following text. Use the notes to help you.

Rob could not decide which of the two girls he liked best. . .

NOTES

Helen: similar to him; same interests; nice personality; old friend of his; older than him; sensible; pretty; in love with him.
Susan: very different from him; an unusual person; strange, fascinating personality; very intelligent; much younger than him; not as pretty as Helen; very beautiful eyes; probably not in love with him.

4 Write a few sentences about one of the following subjects.

1. Compare yourself and a person you know well.
2. What are the differences between people in the north and the south (or the east and the west) of your country?
3. Compare people from your country with the British or the Americans.

Asking and offering

A Buying things

1 Put in suitable words or expressions.

1. I'd .... a shampoo for dry ...., please.
2. ...., medium or small?
3. 'How .... is that?' '65p.'
4. Can I .... round?
5. 'Can I help you?' 'I'm .... served, thank you.'
6. .... I have .... aspirins, please?
7. '........................ else?' 'No, thank you. That's ....'

2 Match the things and their descriptions.

shoe polish	things for keeping hands warm
skis	stuff for sticking things
gloves	a thing for taking pictures
glue	stuff for cleaning shoes
camera	a thing for shaving
razor	things for moving on snow

3 Write descriptions of these things.

a knife ....
....

soap ....
....

toothpaste ....
....

shaving-cream ....
....

a tin opener ....
....

Write descriptions of a few more things.

4 Find out the English names of ten things that you have bought recently. Learn them.

5 Revision. Put in *a*, *some* or *one*.

1. 'Would you like .... cup of tea?' 'Yes, thanks, I'd love ....'
2. Could I have .... shaving-cream, please?
3. 'What colour pen would you like?' '........... red ...., please.'
4. I need .... glue and .... tin of black shoe-polish, please.
5. We're looking for .... fridge.
6. 'Have you got .... packet of washing-powder?' 'I've only got .... small ...., I'm afraid.'

6 Read this with a dictionary.

Housewife Mrs Fay Funnell saved for months to buy a fur coat in the summer sales. Then after queuing for nine days she set fire to the coat – valued at £795 and bought by her in the sale for £79.

Astonished crowds, queuing outside Debenham's in Oxford Street, London, watched as 36-year-old Mrs Funnell burnt the coat.

As every woman's dream disappeared in smoke, she said: 'I am highly delighted. I hate the fur trade because it is cruel to animals. One hundred and fifty minks have died to make this jacket.'

7 Look at the text in Exercise 6. The following expressions are used for the woman who bought the coat: *Housewife Mrs Fay Funnell*; *she*; *her*; *36-year-old Mrs Funnell*; *she*. Can you find and underline the five expressions which are used for the fur coat?

8 Do you think Mrs Funnell was right to burn the coat? (Write two or three sentences.)

I haven't got anything to wear

1 Fill in the blanks. Try to do the exercise *before* you look at the words in the box.

1. 'What's the ....?' 'I'm not feeling very well.' 'Oh, dear. .... I get you an aspirin?'
2. 'Can you .... me some money?' 'Yes, all right, I think .... When can you give it .... to me?'
3. 'Have you .... the time?' 'No, sorry, I'm .... I haven't.'
4. 'Would you like .... to a party this evening?' 'That's very .... of you. I'd love ....' 'All right. Can you .... to my house about eight o'clock?'
5. 'Could I .... one of your dresses?' 'Yes, of course. Do you want .... a pair of shoes to go with it?' 'Well, if you're sure you don't ....'
6. 'Excuse me. .... you tell me the .... to Times Square?' 'I'm sorry. I'm a .... here myself.'
7. 'Have you got .... for a £5 note?' 'Wait a .... I .... have a ....'

afraid	back	borrow	to borrow
change	come	to come	could
got	kind	lend	'll	look
matter	mind	second	shall	so
stranger	to	way		

2 Put in *got* where it is correct.

1. Have you .... a light?
2. Goodbye. Have .... a good holiday.
3. I usually have .... lunch at one o'clock.
4. Excuse me. Have you .... the time?
5. I've .... three brothers.
6. Have you .... a few minutes? I'd like to have .... a talk with you.
7. 'What's the matter?' 'I've .... a headache.'
8. My parents have .... a small farm in Yorkshire.
9. Hello. Nice to see you. Sit down and have .... a drink.
10. She always has .... a bath before she goes to bed.

3 Spelling: double letters. Put another letter in the blank if necessary.

pos**s**ible nec . es**s**ary let . er spel . ing
big . er old . er wait . ing
sit . ing stop . ed rub . ish
definit . ely visit . or

"Not now, Gawain – the neighbours will hear you undressing."

4 **Fill in the blanks in the text with words from the box.**

after again ago because broken called
deep except hit hurt lost only so
soon started stay that walking when

LOST

My sense of direction is not very good, and I easily get .... One day, about ten years ...., I was .... in the mountains between France and Italy .... the weather began to turn bad. I .... to make my way back downhill, ... I did not want to be caught in a storm. But after a few hundred metres I realised .... I was not sure of the way. The clouds came down lower and lower, it started to rain, and .... I was completely lost.

I .... as loud as I could, but of course there was nobody close enough to hear me. I did not want to .... on the mountain, but it was impossible to go on, ... I crawled into a hole between two rocks and waited for the storm to go over. .... two or three hours the rain stopped and the clouds lifted, and I was able to start walking .... I was very cold and hungry, and I had nothing to eat .... a few sweets.

About half an hour later I suddenly recognised my surroundings, and I realised that I was .... two or three hundred metres above the campsite. However, my troubles were not over. On my way down I slipped and .... my knee against a rock. There was a .... cut and it .... very badly, and as soon as I got back to the camp I went to see a doctor. Fortunately, nothing was ....

5 **Write about a time when you were lost, or write a story about somebody who was lost. Use words and expressions from Exercise 4, and from the text about Juliana Koepke on page 14 of the Student's Book.**

"Have you seen a lady without me?"

The future

A Their children will have blue eyes

1 **Where will you be this time tomorrow? This time next week? A month from now? This time next year?**

This time tomorrow I will be ....

This time next ....

A month ....

This ....

2 **Write sentences with *will certainly, will probably, may, will probably not* or *will certainly not*.**
Example:
I will probably not be in the same house in ten years' time.

1. Will you be in the same house in ten years' time?
   ....
2. Will you live to be 100 years old?
   ....
3. Will next year be better for you than this year?
   ....
4. Will it rain this evening?
   ....
5. Will you do all the exercises in this book?
   ....
6. Will you sleep well tonight?
   ....
7. Will you get a lot of presents on your birthday?
   ....
8. Will you climb a mountain during the next 12 months?
   ....
   ....
9. Will doctors discover a cure for cancer before the year 2000?
   ....
   ....
10. Will there be a world war in the next ten years? (Start '*There will/may...*')
   ....

3 Revision. Fill in the table of irregular verbs. Learn the ones you don't know.

INFINITIVE	PAST TENSE	PAST PARTICIPLE
become	became	become
begin	....	....
bring	....	....
build	....	....
buy	....	....
catch	....	....
choose	....	....
come	....	....
cost	....	....
cut	....	....
draw	....	....
dream	....	....
drink	....	....
drive	....	....
eat	....	....
fly	....	....
forget	....	....
give	....	....
go	....	....
put	....	....
wake	....	....

4 Here are some recent predictions about things that may happen in the future. Read them with a dictionary, and decide which developments will do most good to the world. Write down the letters of the predictions in order of importance.

A. If people take a special drug, they will be able to eat as much as they like without getting fat.
B. There will be a vaccine which will prevent tooth decay.
C. There will be drugs which will stop us feeling pain without making us unconscious.
D. Doctors will be able to repair damaged spinal cords.
E. People will be able to live 20–40 years longer than now.
F. Women will be able to have children at the age of 60.
G. We may be able to partly control the weather.
H. Trains will be able to travel at 2,000kph in special vacuum tunnels.

Order of importance: 1...... 2...... 3...... 4...... 5......
6...... 7...... 8......

"You'll wait for me and try to be faithful? Dammit – I'm only in for 30 days."

5 Strange but true. Read this with a dictionary.

About 5,700 stars can be seen on a clear night without a telescope.
If you live in an old house in the country, you may be sharing your house with up to 3,000 animals and insects.
A mole takes about eight hours to tunnel 100 metres.
Diamonds and coal are made of the same chemical element.
Baby whales increase their weight by ten pounds an hour.
During a lifetime, a person's heart pumps enough blood to fill the fuel tanks of 2,100 Boeing 747s.
You get taller when you are asleep.
There were ten days in the ancient Egyptian week.
The silk made by spiders is stronger than steel.

"You'll like Mum and Dad – they're out!"

How about Thursday?

1 Complete the conversation.

SARAH: Hello, Steve. .... is Sarah. How are you?

STEVE: OK. .... about you?

SARAH: Oh, I'm fine. Listen, Steve. I'm ....ing to arrange a party for the weekend. Are you .... on Sunday?

STEVE: Saturday? Well, it's a .... difficult. I'm .... Ann and her family in the evening.

SARAH: No, Sunday.

STEVE: Oh, I'm sorry. I .... Saturday. Sunday might be OK. It .... time?

SARAH: Oh, any time after eight.

STEVE: I can't .... eight, but I'll come .... a bit .... Say, nine?

SARAH: That's fine. Any time you like.

STEVE: Where?

SARAH: My .... Bring a bottle.

STEVE: OK. Thanks very .... See you then.

SARAH: Bye.

2 Put in the right prepositions: *in*, *on*, *at*, *before* or *until*.

1. 'When's your birthday?' '.................... two weeks.'
2. I'll see you again .... Tuesday.
3. I'll be on holiday from tomorrow .... the end of August.
4. Goodnight. See you .... the morning.
5. I must finish this letter .... four o'clock, or I'll miss the post.
6. Hurry up – it'll be time to go .... ten minutes.
7. The next meeting will be .... June 20th.
8. I'll be late for work .... Monday – I've got to go to the dentist.
9. 'Can I speak to Janet?' 'I'm afraid she's away .... next week.'
10. The train leaves .... half an hour.
11. Could you look after the children .... supper time?
12. I'm seeing the dentist .... ten o'clock.

3 Imagine that you are doing some of these things tomorrow. Say how long they will take you. Example:

It will take me half an hour to wash my hair.

wash your hair write to your mother
clean the kitchen make a cake
do your ironing wash your car
pack your suitcase go to the station
run 1,500 metres drive 20km
play three sets of tennis
learn 20 irregular verbs

4 What are you doing next weekend?

....

....

....

....

....

5 **Try the crossword.**

ACROSS

1. 'Where are you from?' 'Germany.' '............ in Germany?'
7. 'Can I speak to Mike?' 'I'm sorry. I'm afraid he's .... in.'
8. Flying machine.
10. All right.
11. Have you made any ....s for the holidays yet?
12. Rubbish!
14. 'What are your ....?' 'Sport, music and travel.'

DOWN

1. You and I.
2. A quarter of twice twenty-two.
3. You're reading one.
4. I'll be here .... six o'clock.
5. Part of your foot.
6. There's a .... light in the sky.
9. 'Where did you have lunch?' 'At the pub round the ....'
11. Things to write with.
12. The opposite of *yes.*
13. Come in and .... down.

(Solution on page 142.)

Unit 7

Things that have happened

A Have you ever...?

1 **Put the correct verb form in each sentence.**

1. When I was a child, I .... cheese. (*never eat*)
2. .... you ever .... alone? (*live*)
3. Thousands of women .... in factories during the Second World War. (*work*)
4. .... you ever .... a passport when you were a child? (*have*)
5. Jaime lives in Venezuela; he .... snow. (*never see*)
6. When your mother was at school, ... she .... to wear a uniform? (*have*)
7. I .... to England in 1980. (*come*)
8. What .... your father .... you for your last birthday? (*give*)
9. Shakespeare .... to university. (*never go*)
10. .... Napoleon ever .... to China? (*ever go*)

2 Write the contractions.

1. The car **will not** start. ....won't........
2. **She has** never been to Europe. ....
3. **She is** nearly 18. ....
4. I think **John is** hungry. ....
5. **I will** tell you tomorrow. ....
6. **I would** like a holiday. ....
7. Pat **has not** telephoned. ....
8. I **cannot** understand it. ....

Write the full forms.

1. It **doesn't** matter. ....does not........
2. **Alan's** six feet tall. ....
3. **She's** very thirsty. ....
4. He says **he'll** pay. ....
5. I **won't** go alone. ....
6. **She's** never met him ....
7. You **mustn't** worry. ....
8. **We'd** like a table for two. ....

3 Write eight or more sentences about yourself. You can choose some of these ideas, or choose other items for yourself.

Do you feel strongly about any political question?
Have you ever done something that surprised your family or friends?
Have you changed very much in the past few years?
How important is cooking and eating food to you?
Is there a certain sort of music, or book, or other entertainment, that you like very much?
Were you happy or unhappy as a child?
Have your parents been an important influence in your life?
Have you ever been in love?

4 Can you fill in the labels with words from the box? Use your dictionary to help you.

armchair bookcase carpet ceiling
chair curtain door fireplace floor
lamp light piano picture plant stereo
switch table wall window

5 **Read one or both of these texts, and do the exercise(s). You can use a dictionary.**

A

(Dick Francis writes 'thrillers' – novels about crime and violence – that take place in the world of British horse racing.)

Dick Francis can't remember learning to ride: it came to him as naturally as learning to walk. Born in South Wales in 1920, he was a child star at horse shows and after six years' service in the RAF during the Second World War, he made his entry into racing as an amateur jockey, becoming a professional National Hunt jockey in 1948. He rode for the Queen Mother and in 1953–4 was Champion Jockey.

Retiring in 1957, Dick Francis became racing correspondent for the *Sunday Express* and began writing. His first book, published that same year, was his autobiography, *The Sport of Queens*, which has recently been revised and updated. This was followed by a number of thrillers, the material for which he has gleaned principally from the racing world. *Forfeit* was awarded the Edgar Allan Poe Mystery Prize for the best crime story of 1969 in America. *Whip Hand* won the 1980 Crime Writers Association Gold Dagger award.

He lives on the edge of the Berkshire Downs with his wife Mary, who helps with the research. He still rides regularly. (from *Enquiry* by Dick Francis)

When you have read the text, put the pictures in the correct order.

Answer: 1............ 2............ 3............
4............ 5............ (Answer on page 142.)

B

Bernard and François Baschet are brothers. They live in Paris and work with new sounds and shapes for making music. They haven't always done this, though; for a long time Bernard managed a factory and François ran a business in Argentina. Then, about 30 years ago, they took their savings and began the work they do now. First they learnt all about how classical musical instruments were made, and then they began inventing their own instruments.

Now their lives are quite varied. They are still inventing new instruments; but Bernard has begun working with children as well. He helps them to discover music without having to read written notes. He sometimes travels, too, giving concerts on his instruments with other musicians. François also travels – sometimes to set up exhibitions, sometimes just for the pleasure of arriving in a new place.

Bernard's main complaint? The telephone. 'When an artist is working,' he says, 'and he has to run to the telephone, something is broken inside. I agree with the sculptor who said that freedom for the artist means having a secretary.'

Which is the most accurate summary of the text?

1. Bernard and François Baschet have spent a large part of their lives making new kinds of musical instruments.
2. The Baschet brothers both work at inventing new musical instruments and teaching children to play them.
3. Bernard and François Baschet have recently begun working with new musical instruments: they invent them, teach children to play them, give concerts and set up exhibitions.

Answer: .... (Answer on page 142.)

B Here is the news

1 **Look at the pictures. What has just happened in each one?**

The boy has just broken the window.

2 **Look at the pictures. What has the person been doing in each one?**

She has been writing letters.

3 Put *since* or *for* into the gaps.

since 1968
since Monday
for two months
.... three hours
.... a long time
.... my birthday
.... last year
for twenty years
.... three days
.... August
.... ten o'clock
.... yesterday
.... two weeks
.... a few minutes

4 Answer these questions with *since* or *for*.

Example: How long have you had the shoes that you are wearing now? for three months

1. How long have you lived at your present address?

   ....

2. How long have you known your English teacher?

   ....

3. How long have you been learning English?

   ....

4. How long have you had this book?

   ....

5. How long have you been doing this exercise?

   ....

5 Match the beginnings and ends (you can use a dictionary) and write out the complete descriptions.

A ruin is	somebody who has grown up.
An adult is	somebody who has beaten everybody else at a sport.
A flood is	somebody who has had an accident.
A graduate is	somebody who has finished university.
A champion is	a child who has lost both parents.
Ice is	water that has covered the land.
An orphan is	a building that has fallen down.
A failure is	water that has frozen.
A casualty is	somebody who has not succeeded in life.

A ruin is a building that has fallen down.

....

....

....

....

....

....

....

....

....

6 **Has your life changed in any important ways since you were a child? Use *used to* and the present perfect. Example:**

I used to be shy, but I have become more self-confident.

7 **Put the words into five groups, according to stress. The first word is done for you.**

above, classical, consulate, remember, insurance, cousin, computer, confirm, cancel, machine, introduce, visitor, foreign, explain, useful, offer, universe, unconscious, believe, happy, guarantee, similar, answer

Oo	oO	Ooo	oOo	ooO
	above			

Know before you go

A Going to Britain

1 **Complete these sentences using *may*.**

1. If a small child plays with matches, *he or she may get burnt.*
2. If you don't lock your car when you park it, ...
   ....
3. If you don't put your name on your suitcase when you travel, ...
   ....
4. If you drive after drinking too much alcohol, ...
   ....
5. If you give a coin to a baby, ...
   ....
6. If you smoke in bed, ...
   ....
7. If a child walks around with a pencil in its mouth, ...
   ....

"Pardon me, we're from New Orleans – would you call this foggy?"

2 **Imagine you are travelling to Britain. Fill in this form.**

LANDING CARD
Immigration Act 1971

Please complete clearly in BLOCK CAPITALS
Veuillez remplir lisiblement en LETTRES MAJUSCULES
Por favor completar claramente en MAYUSCULAS

Family name / Nom de famille / Apellidos ....

Forenames / Prénoms / Nombre(s) de Pila .... **Sex** / Sexe **(M,F)** / Sexo

Date of birth / Date de naissance / Fecha de nacimiento — Day | Month | Year — **Place of birth** / Lieu de naissance / Lugar de nacimiento ....

Nationality / Nationalité / Nacionalidad .... **Occupation** / Profession / Profesión ....

Address in United Kingdom / Adresse en Royaume Uni / Dirección en el Reino Unido ....

....

Signature / Signature / Firma .... MC 011 659

For official use / Réservé usage officiel / Para uso oficial

CAT | –16 | CODE | NAT | POL

IS28FS

3 Invent the other half of this conversation.

IMMIGRATION OFFICER: Good morning. Can I see your passport and landing card, please?

MS CUERVO: ....

OFFICER: How long are you planning to stay in Britain?

MS CUERVO: ....

OFFICER: And the people you're staying with? Are they friends?

MS CUERVO: ....

OFFICER: How much money have you brought for your stay?

MS CUERVO: ....

OFFICER: Yes, well, that looks fine. *(Stamps passport.)* Have a pleasant stay in Britain.

4 Revision: *by* or *on*? Put the words from the box into the correct list.

boat air bus car train foot motorbike horseback underground bicycle

BY	ON
boat	foot
....	....
....	....
....	....
....	....
....	....
....	....
....	....

Now complete the table.

1. travel by air = fly
2. travel .... car = ...
3. travel .... foot = ...
4. travel .... horseback = ...
5. travel .... bicycle = ...

5 Which one is different? Why?

1. coach car bicycle bus

....

2. train bicycle car motorbike

....

3. train car plane bus

....

4. walk ride hitchhike cycle

....

Unit 8A

6 Read the directions and draw the route on the map.

WALK TO LONDON'S MUSEUMS

This walk starts at busy Marble Arch. Go west along the side of Hyde Park, parallel with Bayswater Road, as far as the pleasant water-gardens at the north end of the Serpentine. Walk south across the gardens, then continue down a tree-lined avenue (you are now in Kensington Gardens) to the elaborate Albert Memorial, built between 1864 and 1876 as a monument to Queen Victoria's beloved Prince Consort. The huge brick-coloured building across the road is the Royal Albert Hall, used broadmindedly (and at different times) for events as different as classical music concerts and wrestling matches. Turn right into Kensington Road and cross the road into Queen's Gate, then turn left into Prince Consort Road. Here you see the back of the Albert Hall and part of Imperial College and the Royal College of Music. Turn right into Exhibition Road. Two hundred yards along you will reach the Science Museum, one of the great museums which owe their existence to the profits of the Great Exhibition of 1851. Beyond the Science Museum, which is especially recommended for children who are interested in seeing how things work, are the Natural History Museum and the Geological Museum. Across Exhibition Road is the most famous of the four, the Victoria and Albert Museum.

Walking time to the museums is about an hour.

At least two hours should be allowed for each of the museums you want to visit. Those not wanting to visit the museums can walk along Brompton Road into the smart shopping area of Knightsbridge (Harrods is there). Museum-goers will do better to take a bus when they emerge into the daylight.

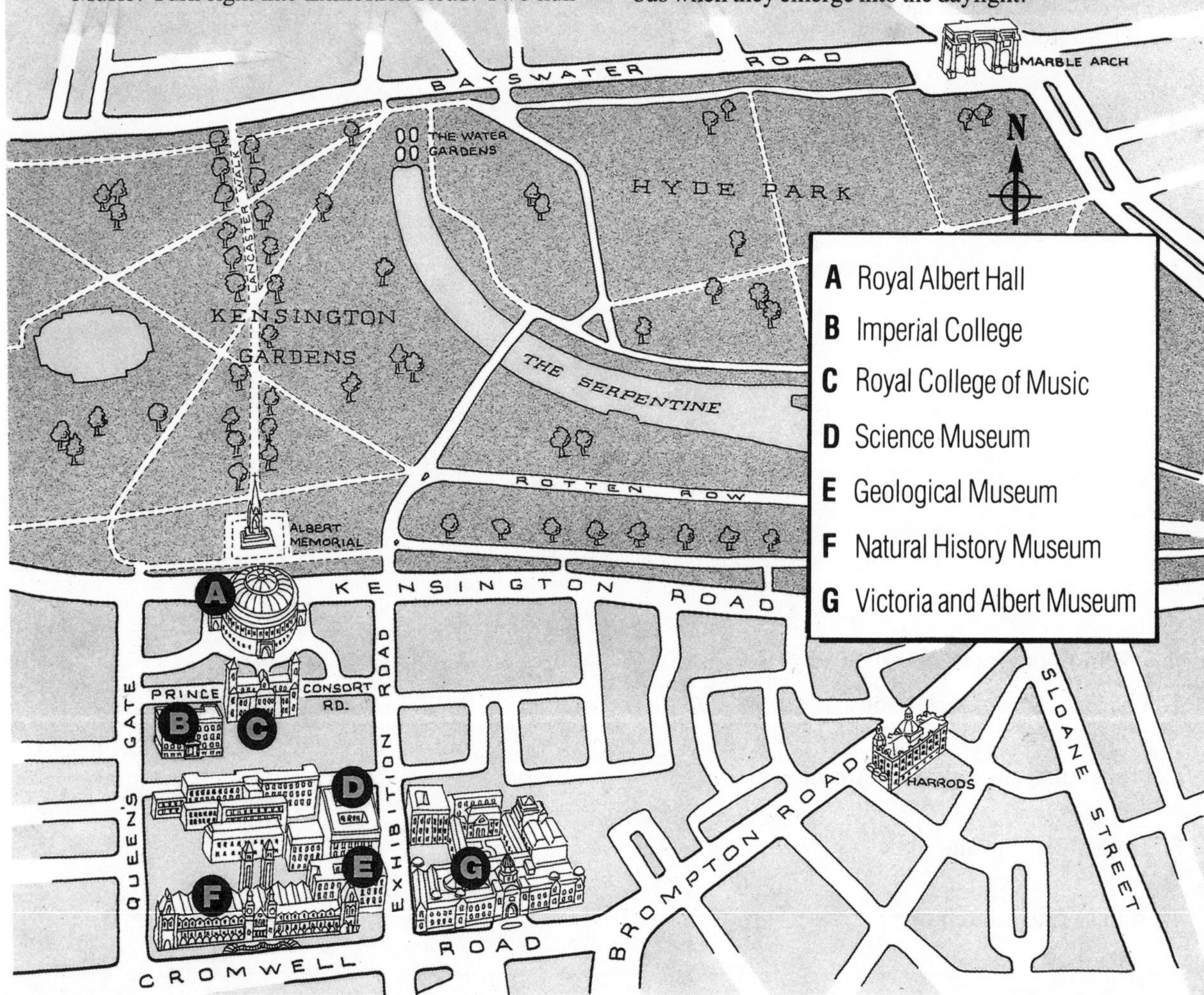

B Going to the USA

1 Put ten of these words into the blanks in the story.

distances fare passport foreign coach reverse-charge choice expensive pickpocket wallet free

When I was 20, I went to the United States. I wanted to see as much of the States as I could, and I didn't have much money. Travelling by plane was too ...., so I decided to travel by .... It was cheap but tiring. The .... in the US are much longer than you realise – I had to sit for a long time to get from one place to another. It was not always boring, though: Americans are very friendly to people who come from ....countries, and I often had interesting conversations with my fellow travellers. Several times I was invited to people's homes for the night, and so I got .... meals and didn't have to pay for a hotel.

One Saturday I was at the coach station in Austin,Texas, when my .... and traveller's cheques were stolen. Luckily my .... was in another pocket, so I didn't have to go to all the trouble of finding the nearest British consulate. I made a .... call to my brother to ask him to cancel my traveller's cheques immediately; but then I didn't know what to do. I couldn't get new traveller's cheques until the following Monday, and I only had enough change to buy myself a cup of coffee. I decided to do that and try to think things out. In the café I started talking to a student and told him about my problem. He said he would lend me some money and invited me to stay with him until Monday. He seemed to be a nice person, which was lucky, because I really had no .... As it happened, we got on very well; we write to one another regularly and he has come to visit me in England. So a .... found a new American friend for me.

2 *Should* or *will have to?*

1. If you want to go to China, you .... get a visa.
2. If you want to go to China, you .... learn Chinese.
3. If you go to Rome, you .... go to St Peter's – it's beautiful.
4. If you go to St Peter's, you .... wear suitable clothes; if you don't, the guards won't let you in.
5. If you go to Brazil, you .... go through immigration control.
6. If you go to Brazil, you .... make sure you see Brasilia.

Now imagine an American woman wants to come to spend a year in your country. What will she have to do? What should she do? Write five or more sentences.

3 In English, most two-syllable words are stressed on the first syllable, like this:

□□ passport   □□ airline

Can you find the two words in this list that are stressed on the second syllable?

campsite distance foreign hotel village country journey sometimes often airline wallet passport customs arrive likely

Now group these three-syllable words according to their stress patterns.

exciting beautiful underground embassy consulate agreement insurance example telephone accident discover comfortable

□□□	□□□
beautiful	*exciting*
....	....
....	....
....	....
....	....
....	....
....	....

Unit 8B

4 **Put capital letters and punctuation marks where they belong.**

one of my friends has just returned from a holiday in the usa he now considers himself an expert on the states it makes me laugh but it s not the first time i ve seen it people go to america with a firm idea of what they re going to find there and then they find it they don t meet many americans because they never leave their own little group they go to the tourist traps disneyland and miami beach for example and follow their tour guides around like sheep they are shown exactly what they want to see and so they think that america really is exactly like its cinema image

i think the only way to get to know a country is to go there alone or in a very small group and to stay in a place where there are not very many tourists then you have a chance of meeting people and finding out what their life is really like of course it is important to try and learn at least a little bit of the language before you go you won t come back an expert but you will know more than my friend knows about america

---

Unit 9

Problems

Emergency

1 ***Is* or *has*? Write the correct form.**

1. There's a woman in your office. There is ....
2. There's been a fire at the airport. ....
3. My husband's fallen down the stairs. ....
4. My wife's working in Edinburgh this week. ....
5. Somebody's on the phone right now. ....
6. There's been a mistake. ....
7. She's broken her finger. ....
8. He's going to speak later. ....
9. Somebody's stolen my bicycle. ....
10. There's a post office very near here. ....
11. My son's hurt. ....
12. My daughter's broken your pen; I'm very sorry. ....

2 **Write what people should do in these emergencies. You can use a dictionary.**

1. I think her leg is broken. Don't move her. Phone for an ambulance.
2. I can hear terrible screaming from the flat upstairs. ....
3. My passport has been stolen. ....
4. I can't turn the water off in the bathroom. The floor is covered with water. ....
5. There's a fire in the corridor, and I'm on the fifth floor. ....
6. My friend's poured boiling water on her hand. ....
7. There's been a car accident. A man is hurt. He can't get out of the car. ....
8. I can smell a lot of gas in my flat. ....

3 Read these extracts from a radio report and choose the correct verb forms.

'People *have come* / *came* from all over Britain for this demonstration. I would say there are about 30,000 people here. Some of the demonstrators from Scotland *have left* / *left* home shortly after midnight last night to arrive here on time.

All of the members of one group *have painted* / *painted* their hands and faces purple and are wearing gas masks. Others *have brought* / *brought* their children; one child is carrying a sign saying "Don't forget us!"

The police *have arrived* / *arrived* early this morning, and have been waiting since then in case of trouble. One of the groups opposing the march *have made* / *made* a statement yesterday saying that they would do all they could to disturb the demonstration, so police officials are being very careful.

The march seems very well-organised; organisers *have just given* / *just gave* armbands to volunteers, who will make sure that people stay on the authorised route and remain peaceful.

Wait a moment. I *have just had* / *just had* a report that a dangerous-looking parcel has been found under one of the organisers' cars. Police *have taken* / *took* the parcel and are taking it to a bomb disposal van.'

(A few minutes later) 'Oh, no! The bomb *has exploded* / *exploded*; people are running and screaming; several people, including some children, seem to be hurt, but I can't tell how badly.'

(A few minutes later) 'Police *have called* / *called* for the organisers; other policemen and -women are clearing a path for the ambulances.'

(A few minutes later) 'The police *have finished* / *finished* talking to the organisers now. I will try to get a statement from one of them... Yes, here is Amanda Raines, one of the organisers of the demonstration. She *has just spoken* / *just spoke* with the police. When do you think the bomb *has been planted* / *was planted*, Amanda?'

'We *have arrived* / *arrived* here last night at ten o'clock and *have slept* / *slept* in the vans. The car where the bomb was found has not been moved since then. Someone *has probably planted* / *probably planted* the bomb while we were asleep; the police *have told* / *told* me that it looks like a time bomb.

'Do you think the bomb *has been planted* / *was planted* by the opposition group?'

'I think we must wait until we have more information. The group said they would disturb the demonstration, but we cannot hold them responsible just because of that.'

4 Grammar revision. 'Reply questions' are a way of showing interest when someone speaks to you. Write the correct reply question for each sentence, and add another sentence to keep the conversation going.

1. I've just bought a new car. Have you? What kind?
2. My sister works in the same place as your wife. ....
3. I've passed my exam! ....
4. Deidre's just had a baby. ....
5. I'll help you with that if you want. ....
6. I went to Morocco last year. ....
7. I'm leaving my job at the end of the month. ....
8. My brother was in Ethiopia at the same time as you were. ....
9. John had a terrible car accident last week. ....
10. I was at school with the Prime Minister. ....
11. My wife's running in the Boston Marathon this year. ....
12. James has just changed jobs. ....

5 **Try to understand this text by looking up only the words you need in the dictionary. You should not look up more than eight words.**

THAMES FLOODING
Don't wait until it happens.
If you live, work or travel in London you should learn your Thames flood drill now.
GLC
Working for London
FIRST PUBLIC WARNING
About four hours before flooding, warnings will be issued on radio, TV and by public notices. Two hours after the first public warning bus, underground and rail services will start to be withdrawn.
Wherever you are GO HOME IMMEDIATELY
even if home is in the risk area.
LAST PUBLIC WARNING-sirens
About one hour before flooding sirens will sound in the flood risk area. No trains or buses will be running in the risk area.
DO NOT TRAVEL IN THE FLOOD RISK AREA
Everyone in the danger area should MOVE TO A HIGHER FLOOR or follow the advice of the local town hall.
Stay tuned to local radio
CAPITAL (194 medium wave, 95.8 VHF)
LBC (261 medium wave; 97.3 VHF)
RADIO LONDON (206 medium wave; 94.9 VHF)
38761

Check the words you looked up against the list on page 142.

B You made me do it

1 **Read these sentences with the correct stress.**

I **did**n't **mean** to **do** it.
I for**got what** I was **do**ing.
It **does**n't **mat**ter.
We can **get** a **new one.**
I **did**n't **do** it on **pur**pose.
It was an **ac**cident.

2 **Write sentences about things that make you happy, unhappy, sleepy, angry, tired.**
Example:

My family makes me happy.

3 Answer these questions. Use *make* in your answers.

1. What do sunlight and water do for flowers?
2. What do aspirins do when you have a headache?
3. What do customs officers sometimes make people do?
4. What does very hot water do to woollen clothes?
5. What are three things that your parents or teachers made you do when you were a child?

4 *Since, for,* or *ago*? Put the correct word into each sentence. Examples:

We've been in this village *for* four years.
I used to swim pretty well, but that was years *ago*.
She was married *for* ten years, but she's been living on her own *since* 1982.

1. 'When did you start working on this project?' 'Oh, about three years.'
2. My brother's been married Christmas, and he only wrote to me about it a week.
3. How long did you order the dress?
4. I've wanted to go to Vienna ever I was a child.
5. Running has been a popular sport in the United States several years now.
6. 'Have you been here long?' 'No, we got here about five minutes.'
7. I've had this cough January.
8. Britain has had a National Health Service the end of the Second World War.

5 Read this conversation, and then write a story about it like the one in Exercise 4 in the Student's Book.

STEVE: Come on, Andrew! Time to leave for school!
ANDREW: Er, I'm not quite ready, Dad.
STEVE: (*going up to Andrew's room*) Not quite ready?! You haven't even started getting dressed! I sent you up here twenty minutes ago – what the hell have you been doing?
ANDREW: Er, reading.
STEVE: Well, I'm delighted you enjoy reading, but this is not the time for it. Now hurry up. Come on, you can button your shirt and put on your tie and jacket in the car. Come *on*, Andrew, we're going to be late!
(*In the car*)
STEVE: I'll never get to work on time now; Mr Lewis will be furious.
ANDREW: Er, Dad, I can't put my jacket on with my seat belt fastened.
STEVE: Well, take your damn seat belt off for a minute! Kids!
ANDREW: Dad! Look out! The light!
(*Squeal of brakes*)
STEVE: Damn! Oh my God, let's see your head. Does it hurt very badly?
ANDREW: Not an awful lot, no.
STEVE: I *am* sorry, Andrew. We'll ask them to put a plaster on it when we get to school. I shouldn't have told you to take your seat belt off.
ANDREW: That's all right, Dad.

6 **Try the crossword.**

(Solution on page 142.)

ACROSS

1. It makes a car go faster.
7. Boy child.
8. Sorry – I didn't do it on ....
10. I'll see you .... Tuesday.
12. She lives with .... mother in a big house in the country.
14. 'It's broken.' 'It doesn't ....'
16. Telephone me .... four o'clock.
18. You can keep money in it.
20. All right.
21. It can make you feel happy.
22. Love is all you ....

DOWN

2. People who have colds sometimes do this.
3. The opposite of import.
4. Today's not as cold .... yesterday.
5. 'Come and have a drink.' 'No, I don't want ....'
6. Three plus eight minus four plus two minus six plus two minus four.
9. The opposite of *off*.
11. It makes a car stop.
13. He .... too much: he'll get fat.
14. Sorry – I didn't .... to do it.
15. I don't want it – please .... it away.
17. The same as 20.
19. North-east.

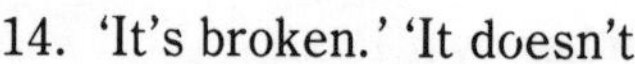

"Pay attention to the game, will you!"

If and when

A If you see a black cat,...

1 *If* or *when*?

1. .... I get rich one day, I'll buy myself a Rolls Royce.
2. The house is so big – it's a bit frightening at night .... it's dark.
3. I suppose I'll have more time to myself .... the children get older.
4. .... it rains this afternoon, we won't have to water the flowers this evening.
5. .... a stranger offers you a lift home from school in his car, just say 'No, thank you' and walk straight on.
6. My mother is going to move to the country .... she retires.
7. .... I live to be 100, I'd like to have an enormous party.
8. You'll feel much better tomorrow .... you go to bed early tonight.
9. .... you go to bed tonight, could you leave the kitchen light on?
10. I don't think life will be worth living .... there is a third world war.
11. We'll have an easier time with money after November, ... we finish paying for the car.
12. Monica usually brings her cat .... she comes to visit us.

2 Put in the correct verb tenses.

1. I will come and see you tomorrow if I have time. (*come*; *have*)
2. I will phone you when I arrive. (*phone*; *arrive*)
3. If it .... a warm night, we .... the party in the garden. (*be*; *have*)
4. Do you think you .... a job when you .... school? (*find*; *leave*)
5. If you .... hungry, tell me and I .... you something to eat. (*be*; *get*)
6. If you .... me the keys, I .... your car round to the front door. (*give*; *bring*)
7. When I .... time, I .... myself some new clothes. (*have*; *buy*)
8. If it .... at the weekend, we .... at home. (*rain*; *stay*)
9. If Mother .... on Sunday, I .... a lemon meringue pie. (*come*; *make*)
10. When I .... work, I .... round the world. (*stop*; *travel*)

3 **Grammar revision. Complete the table of irregular verbs.**

PRESENT	PAST	PAST PARTICIPLE
bleed	........bled........	........bled........
....	broke	....
....	....	burnt
fall	....	....
get	....	....
....	hit	....
hurt	....	....
mean	....	....
....	....	seen
spill	....	....
....	....	stolen
....	threw	....

4 **Spelling revision. Write the contractions.**

1. I am ....I'm........
   you are ....
   he is ....
   she is ....
   it is ....
   we are ....
   they are ....
2. I am not ....
   you are not ....
   he is not ....
3. there is ....
   there is not ....
4. do not ....
   does not ....
5. did not ....
6. have not ....
   has not ....
7. I will ....
   you will ....
   he will ....
   she will ....
   it will ....
   we will ....
   they will ....
   John will ....
8. cannot ....
9. I would like ....
10. should not ....

5 **Revision. Choose words from this list to put in the blanks: *me, you, him, her, us, them, myself, yourself, himself, herself, ourselves, yourselves, themselves.***

1. Could you lend .... your watch?
2. 'Why are you talking to ....?' 'Because nobody else will listen to me.'
3. When I looked at .... in the mirror this morning, I realised I looked very tired.
4. 'What do you think of the Harrisons?' 'I don't like .... much'.
5. We had a lovely time in Wales. We enjoyed .... enormously.
6. Please write soon and give .... your phone number.
7. I prefer to listen to music by ....
8. Do you do the housework ...., or does somebody do it for ....?
9. 'What's the matter with Mary's leg?' 'She hurt .... when she was skiing.'
10. If you see John, give .... my love.
11. Paul's only two and a half, but he can nearly dress ....

6 A word can have several meanings. An important part of using a dictionary is choosing which meaning is used in the text you are reading. For each of the words defined, circle the meaning which fits the text best.

LOVE IS AN INSIDE-OUT NIGHTIE

Girls! Here's a great way to find out the name of your future husband.

According to an old superstition, you will dream of your husband-to-be if you –

Wear your nightie inside out.

OR *sleep with a mirror under your pillow.*

OR *count nine stars each night, for nine nights.*

OR *rub your bedposts with a lemon.*

OR *eat 100 chicken gizzards.*

OR *fill your mouth with water and run three times round the houses.*

The first man you see as you run will have the same name as your future spouse.

If you don't believe me, ask researcher Alvin Schwartz.

He's about to publish a book called Cross Your Fingers, Spit In Your Hat – a collection of the superstitions and odd customs people use to help them through life.

And he has found that we're just as anxious to court Lady Luck as any other generation.

We don't just believe old wives' tales – we're busy making up new ones.

Mr Schwartz says: 'We rely on superstitions for the same reasons people always have.

When we are faced with situations we cannot control – which depend on luck or chance – superstitions make us feel more secure.'

(John Hill, *Sun*)

nightie: night-dress
gizzard: part of a bird's digestive system
spouse: marriage partner
superstition: belief in luck, magic, etc.
court: try to get the favour of
old wives' tales: superstitions

Definitions

1
great/greɪt/ *adj* **1** of excellent quality or ability: *the great women of the past|a great king, artist, etc.* **2** [A] important: *a great occasion* **3** large in amount or degree: *Take great care.|It was a great loss to us all.|a great deal|a great many* **4** [A] (of people) unusually active in the stated way: *He's a great talker.|We're great* (= very close) *friends.* **5** [A] (*usu. before another adj of size*) big: *a great (big) tree* **6** *infml* unusually good; very enjoyable: *What a great idea!|This new singer is really great!* **7** great-: **a** being the parent of a person's grandparent: *great-grandfather* **b** being the child of a person's grandchild: *great-granddaughter* **c** being the brother or sister of a person's grandparent: *great-aunt* **d** being the child of a person's nephew or niece: *great-nephew* – **greatness** *n* [U]

2
a·bout[1] /əˈbaʊt/ *prep* **1** on the subject of: *a book about stars* **2** in; through: *They walked about the streets.|books lying about the room|He's somewhere about the house.* **3** *fml* on the body of: *He had a gun hidden* **about his person**. (= in his clothes) **4 what|how about**: **a** what news or plans have you concerning: *What about Jack? We can't just leave him here.* **b** (making a suggestion): *How about a drink?*
about[2] *adv* **1** here and there; in all directions or places; on all sides; around: *They go about together most of the time.|We sat about on the floor.* **2** somewhere near: *Is there anybody about?* **3** a little more or less than: *about five miles|about ten years* **4** so as to face the opposite way **5 be about to** to be just ready to; be going to: *We were about to leave when it started to rain.*

3
odd /ɒd||ɑd/ *adj* **1** strange; unusual: *odd behaviour|an odd person* **2** [A] separated from a pair or set to which it belongs: *an odd shoe* **3** (of a number) that cannot be divided exactly by 2: *1, 3, 5, 7, etc., are odd.* – opposite **even 4** [A] not regular; OCCASIONAL: *He does the odd job for me from time to time.|I only get the odd moment to read.* **5** [after *n*] *infml* (after numbers) with rather more: *20-odd years*

4
cus·tom /ˈkʌstəm/ *n* **1** [C;U] (an) established socially accepted practice: *Social customs vary greatly from country to country.* **2** [C] the habitual practice of a person: *His custom was to get up early and have a cold bath.* **3** [U] *fml* regular support given to a shop by those who buy goods or services: *We lost a great deal of custom when that new shop opened.* **4 custom-** (done) in accordance with the wishes of the buyer (CUSTOMER): *a custom-built car|custom-made clothes* – see HABIT (USAGE)
cus·toms/ˈkʌstəmz/ *n* [P] **1** (*often cap.*) a place where travellers' belongings are searched when leaving or entering a country: *As soon as I'd got through customs I felt at home.* **2** taxes paid on goods entering or leaving a country **3** (*often cap.*) the government organization established to collect these taxes

5
anx·ious/ˈæŋkʃəs/ *adj* **1** |*for, about*| feeling or causing anxiety; troubled: *I was anxious about the children when they didn't come home from school.* **2** [+ *to-v*/*that*/*for*] having a strong wish to do something; eager: *He was anxious to please his guests.* – see NERVOUS (USAGE) – **anxiously** *adv*

(from the *Longman Active Study Dictionary*)

B How to fill a kettle

1 Put in the correct verb form.

1. We .... anything until we hear from you. (*not do*)
2. I'll tell you as soon as I .... (*know*)
3. If I .... George, I'll tell him to come and see you. (*see*)
4. I .... happy when this job is finished. (*be*)
5. What .... if the police find out? (*happen*)
6. It'll be nice when we .... back home again. (*get*)
7. I .... your luggage until you come back. (*look after*)
8. As soon as you know when you want to leave, phone us and we .... a flight for you. (*reserve*)
9. I'm going to take a short holiday when I .... this job. (*finish*)
10. Don't forget to put the lights out when you .... to bed. (*go*)

2 Put *when* or *until* in each blank.

1. Could you let me know .... Ms Amis arrives?
2. I can't give you an answer .... I hear from my bank.
3. .... the post comes, could you see if there's a letter from Emma in it?
4. Could you wait .... the children get home from school?
5. Eric's mother will be staying with us .... Christmas.
6. Who's going to look after your dog .... you go to America?
7. .... you make mayonnaise, you should make sure the oil and the egg are both at the same temperature.
8. Just keep straight on .... you see a big church; then take the first turning on the right.
9. I'll wait for you .... nine o'clock; if you aren't here by then, I'll know you have missed the train.
10. Don't try to get off the train .... it is moving.

'There must be easier ways of killing mice.'

3 Circle the one in each group that is different, and write why.

1. kettle saucepan (plate) frying-pan
   You can cook in the others.
   OR You don't eat out of the others.
2. wheel plate shoe penny
   ....
3. cow pig fish chicken
   ....
4. onion asparagus melon potato
   ....
5. funny sharp hard heavy
   ....
6. middle both side end
   ....
7. stem flower root tree
   ....

(Answers on page 143.)

4 Revision. Put one of the words from the box into each blank.

at	from	in	into	of	off	on
over	through	to	under	with		

1. Do you eat melon .... a spoon or a knife and fork?
2. Ask the bus driver to tell you where to get ....
3. Shall we meet .... the cinema?
4. Concorde flies .... our house twice a day; it makes a terrible noise.
5. Rob jumped .... the swimming pool with all his clothes on – he must have been drunk!
6. Some of the marchers threw stones at the police; one stone went .... the window of a police car, and hit a policewoman on the head.
7. 'Do you know where my keys are?' 'I think they're .... the table .... the kitchen.'
8. A lot .... the people in our village work with horses.
9. We're going .... France for our summer holidays.
10. People .... warm countries generally have a hard time getting used to the winter in England.
11. I didn't see the cat when I walked into the room, because it was .... the bed.

5 **A group of friends living in different countries lent each other their houses for holidays. Debbie and Simon lent their house to Joe and Rosa; Joe and Rosa lent their house to Vincent and Eric; Vincent and Eric lent their house to Barbara and Irene; Barbara and Irene lent their house to Debbie and Simon.**

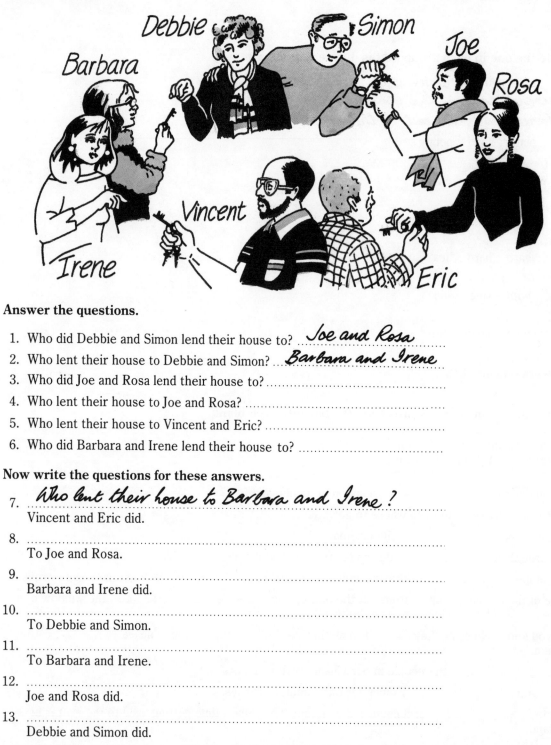

Answer the questions.

1. Who did Debbie and Simon lend their house to? Joe and Rosa
2. Who lent their house to Debbie and Simon? Barbara and Irene
3. Who did Joe and Rosa lend their house to? ....
4. Who lent their house to Joe and Rosa? ....
5. Who lent their house to Vincent and Eric? ....
6. Who did Barbara and Irene lend their house to? ....

Now write the questions for these answers.

7. Who lent their house to Barbara and Irene?
   Vincent and Eric did.
8. ....
   To Joe and Rosa.
9. ....
   Barbara and Irene did.
10. ....
    To Debbie and Simon.
11. ....
    To Barbara and Irene.
12. ....
    Joe and Rosa did.
13. ....
    Debbie and Simon did.

6 **Read this note. Some of the words which help link the first paragraph together are underlined, and the links they make are shown. Underline eight or more other linking words in the note.**

Dear Joe and Rosa,

Welcome to Upton! We hope you will enjoy staying in our house. Mr and Mrs Perry, at number 5 across the street, have an extra set of keys; and they can probably help you with any problems that you run into. Mrs Perry looked after Neil for us before he went to school, and Mr Perry has helped us with some repairs in the house. So they both know the house; and they are very nice people.

A few things you will need to know:

The hot water heater will come on by itself when the water starts getting cold, from 7 to 10 in the morning and from 5 to 11 at night. If you want to change these times, move the little dials in the box above the kitchen sink. You can get two medium-sized baths out of a tank of water, and then you have to wait about 40 minutes for it to heat up again.

To wash clothes, just follow the directions on the washing machine. When it finishes washing, the door stays locked for one minute, so you have to wait to open it. Don't open the door just after programme G (nylons), because the machine will be full of water. Put it on programme H to empty the water.

Useful telephone numbers are on the pad by the phone.

That's about all. Please remember to lock both doors when you go out. I will phone on Tuesday to see if everything is all right. Hope you enjoy your holiday!

All the best,

Debbie

7 **Now imagine some friends will be staying in your house. Write them a note like Debbie's, explaining anything that is important.**

Unit 12

Causes and origins

THERE IS NO PRACTICE BOOK WORK FOR UNIT 11.

From tree to paper

1 **What are you wearing at the moment? What are your clothes made of?**

2 **Grammar revision. Put in *the* if necessary.**

1. Our house was built in ....the.... 15th century.
2. ....–.... paper is made from ....–.... wood.
3. It was invented by .... Chinese.
4. You can travel to .... United States by .... air or by .... sea.
5. .... iron is not as strong as .... steel.
6. 'Do you like this song?' '........... words are stupid, but I like .... music.'
7. 'Would you like a glass of wine?' 'No, thanks, I don't drink .... alcohol.'
8. Could you tell me .... way to .... nearest police station?

3 **Write sentences to say what countries these languages are spoken in.**
Example:

Japanese is spoken in Japan.

Japanese Chinese Arabic German
English Spanish Russian Greek

....

....

....

....

....

....

....

"Hello, wall. Did you have a good day today? My big news is I discovered a new, miracle washday product that has me all excited..."
Heath

4 **Write about three things that are grown or manufactured or produced in your country; add as many details as you can.**

5 **Read the text with a dictionary.**

IRON AND STEEL

Copper and tin were used before iron: they melt at a lower temperature, and can be mixed to form a useful metal called bronze.

Iron was probably first extracted from meteorites, perhaps around 3000 BC. (Iron ornaments dating from 5,000 years ago have been found in the Middle East.) Later, iron was extracted from iron ore (impure iron) by the Hittites, around 2000 BC. The iron was first heated, then hammered to remove the impurities, then cooled. Finally, the iron was heated again and shaped into tools or weapons.

Later, in India first of all, people found out how to make fires hot enough to melt iron (at a temperature of 1,539°C), by driving air through the fuel. This made it possible to produce steel. Steel is made from iron mixed with a little carbon (0.15% – 0.25%). Steel is harder than pure iron, and is less brittle (it does not break as easily). Every motorist is the owner of a ton of steel.

Now put these in the correct order.

a. Hotter fires became possible.
b. People got iron from meteorites.
c. Steel was produced.
d. Bronze was first made.
e. People hit heated ore to get iron.

6 **Write the name of each numbered thing in the picture, and write what it's made of.**

Example:

1. oven – made of steel, iron, glass and plastic.

B Who killed Harrison?

1 **Put the correct form of the verb in each blank.**

1. Last Saturday I was .... to Cambridge to visit a friend, and my wife wanted .... to Reading to run in a marathon. (*go*; *go*)
2. I telephoned the railway station .... what times the trains were. (*find out*)
3. I was .... that the 8.14 train would get me to London in time to reach Cambridge by 10.30. (*tell*)
4. So my wife drove me to the station on her way to Reading, and I was .... on the platform at 8.05. (*stand*)
5. A few minutes later, it was .... that the train was .... to be late. (*announce*; *go*)
6. I knew I was .... to miss my connection in London; but I couldn't phone my friend to tell him because the telephone on the platform was .... (*go*; *break*)
7. Meanwhile, my wife was .... other problems: there were road works on the way to Reading, and the main road was .... (*have*; *close*)
8. After a while she realised that she was lost; she was afraid she was going .... late. (*be*)
9. But she finally .... the sports ground. The gate was .... and there was a big sign saying 'Reading Harriers 2nd Annual Marathon – Sunday August 27th'. (*find*; *lock*)
10. Some days it's a mistake to get out of bed, as my mother used .... (*say*)

2 Look at these examples.

The *Pastoral Symphony* was written **by** Beethoven. (Beethoven wrote it.)

The *Pastoral Symphony* was written **with** a pen made from a goose feather. (Beethoven used a pen made from a goose feather to write it.)

Beethoven's foot was injured **by** a falling stone. (The stone fell by itself.)

Now put *by* or *with* in each sentence.

1. This land was taken from the Apaches .... the white people.
2. Some oriental rugs are made .... very young children.
3. Hollandaise sauce should always be stirred .... a wooden spoon.
4. This letter was written .... a left-handed person.
5. He was knocked down .... a flower pot that fell out of a seventh-floor window.
6. He was hit on the head and face .... a broken chair leg.
7. The cheese was covered .... a damp cloth.
8. I have been asked .... the Prime Minister to make no announcement until we have further information.

3 In a race, the results were as follows:

James beat Olson.
Olson was beaten by Andrews.
Peters was beaten by George and James.
Peters beat Smith.
Andrews was beaten by George, who was beaten by James.
Andrews beat Peters, and so did Olson.

Who won?

(Answer on page 143.)

4 Complete the text with words from the box. Use a dictionary.

added	built	burnt down
damaged	rebuilt	repaired used

Glastrop Cathedral was founded by Henry Morcam in 1442, and was .... between 1443 and 1458. During the Civil War it was .... as a military headquarters, and was badly .... It was .... and restored after the war by Lord Evelyn Fairfax, and a new tower was .... In 1824 part of the cathedral was ....; it was not .... until 1883.

Now read these notes and write a text about the house.

Stroud House: built James Stroud 1676
18th century used as farmhouse
damaged by fire 1776
bought Andrew Scott
repaired, new floor added
badly damaged in World War II
bought National Trust after war
completely rebuilt
opened to public 1968

5 **Revision. Underline the stressed syllables like this:**

America

Circle the letters that are pronounced /ə/, like this:

America

Then put each word under the correct stress pattern. Use your dictionary to help. Try to remember the pronunciation of the words.

advertisement	demonstration	kilometre
American	emergency	participate
apologise	fortunately	reservation
appreciate	immigration	self-confident
calculator	information	supermarket
conversation		

□□□□ (1st stressed)	□□□□ (2nd stressed)	□□□□ (3rd stressed)
....	American	....
....	....	....
....	....	....
....	....	....
....	....	....
....	....	....

6 **Revision. Fill in the table of irregular verbs. Learn the ones you don't know.**

PRESENT	PAST TENSE	PAST PARTICIPLE
speak	spoke	spoken
spell	....	....
spend	....	....
stand	....	....
swim	....	....
take	....	....
teach	....	....
tell	....	....
think	....	....
understand	....	....
wear	....	....
win	....	....
write	....	....

7 **Put one of the expressions from the box in each blank.**

have a talk	have breakfast	have a look
have a dream	have a wonderful time	
have a shower	have a drink	have a baby

1. I'm sure you'll .... in Corsica; we've been there three times and enjoyed it every time.
2. What time do you usually ....?
3. Have you heard the news? Ellen and Jim are going to ....! I'm going to be a grandmother!
4. Sit down and .... while I finish this, and then we can talk.
5. I'm going to have to .... with Brian – I think he's been using our phone to call Australia.
6. I .... sometimes that I'm locked in a small room.
7. I'm so hot and tired! I think I'll .... before I start dinner, if you don't mind.
8. I think I heard the doorbell ring – could you ....?

Now put *have* into the correct tense.

9. Can I phone you back? We .... lunch right now.
10. I .... a conversation with Alison this morning when Jerry came into her office.
11. I .... a day off next Friday, so I'll try to finish this by Thursday.
12. We .... trouble starting the car when it's cold.

8 **Try the crossword.**

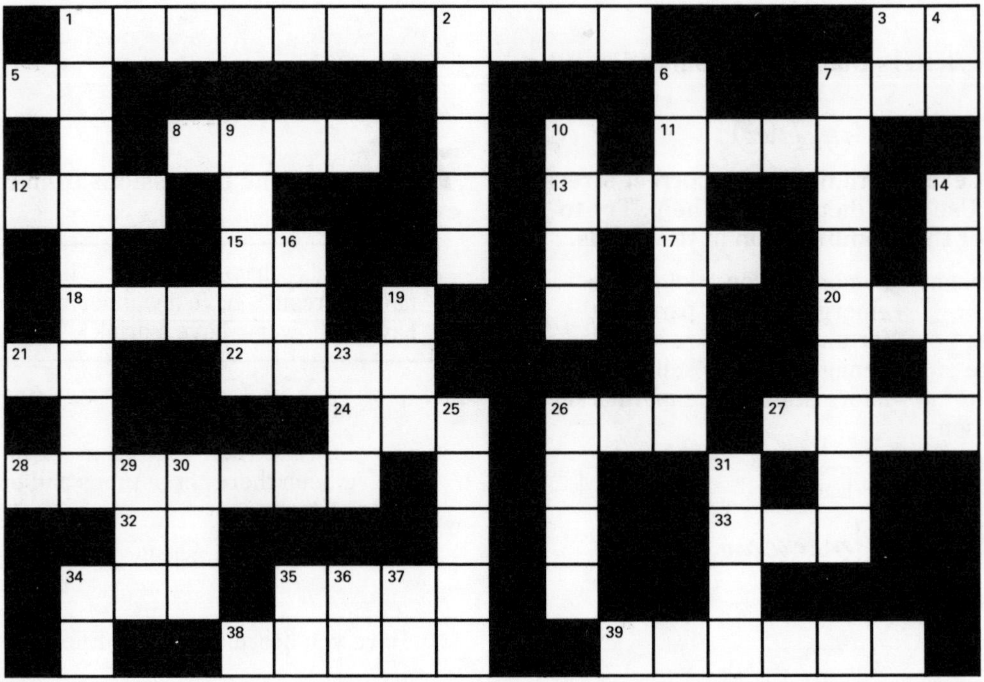

ACROSS

1. This makes the car go faster.
3. Opposite of *from*.
5. In the morning.
7. Neither John .... I speak French.
8. A letter, a visit, a phone ....
11. One less than twice.
12. I'm hungry, ... I'll wait until Pat gets here to eat.
13. Opposite of *in*.
15. Me, you, him, her, ..., us, them.
17. Another sort of hello.
18. The third floor is .... the second floor.
20. Harder than *touch*.
21. A secretary and .... electrician.
22. Could you give one of these to .... child?
24. A colour.
26. Something to put things in.
27. 'When were you ....?' 'On December 17, 1951.'
28. A hundred years.
32. Something to say if you're surprised.
33. You need this to live.
34. Doesn't your sister .... you some money?
35. You use this to mend things.
38. This can have from four to eighteen wheels.
39. Opposite of *youngest*.

DOWN

1. A car, a bus, a lorry, an ....
2. Opposite of *child*.
3. We went .... the Alps for our holidays.
4. Would you like some tea, ... some coffee?
6. Opposite of *everything*.
7. This person lives near you.
9. Not dead.
10. Arms, legs and stomach are part of this.
14. That's the best meal I've ever ....
16. The English drink a lot of it.
19. France, Brazil, ... United States.
23. Opposite of *laugh*.
25. The .... news programme is not as long as the Sunday one.
26. Fire does this.
29. I used to run every day, but .... I only do it two or three times a week.
30. How big is .... sun?
31. By air, by sea, by ....
34. How many .... your cousins live in England?
35. I'll be home from 6 .... 8 this evening.
36. Have you got any sisters .... brothers?
37. Same as *36 down*.

(Solution on page 143.)

Descriptions

A Places

1 **Complete the letter with words and expressions from the box.**

a long way away beautiful camping can fish full islands lake mountains quiet river stream there's woods yards yesterday

Dear Rachel,
This must be one of the most
places in the world.
by a small
We're
(perhaps I should
!)
call it a large
.
that comes down from the
The water is amazingly clear, and it's
of little
. About 300
away it runs
with
into a big
- I swam
lots of
. On
out to one
the other side of the lake
a wonderful view of the Alps - on a clear
see
day you
Mont Blanc, 60 miles away. There are
all round, and
it's very very
and peaceful. Liverpool seems
!
Love to you and the family,
Hilda.

2 **Write a letter from a person who is on holiday, describing the place where he or she is staying. Use some words and expressions from the letter in Exercise 1.**
OR: Describe the view from your bedroom window.
OR: Write about a place that you like very much.

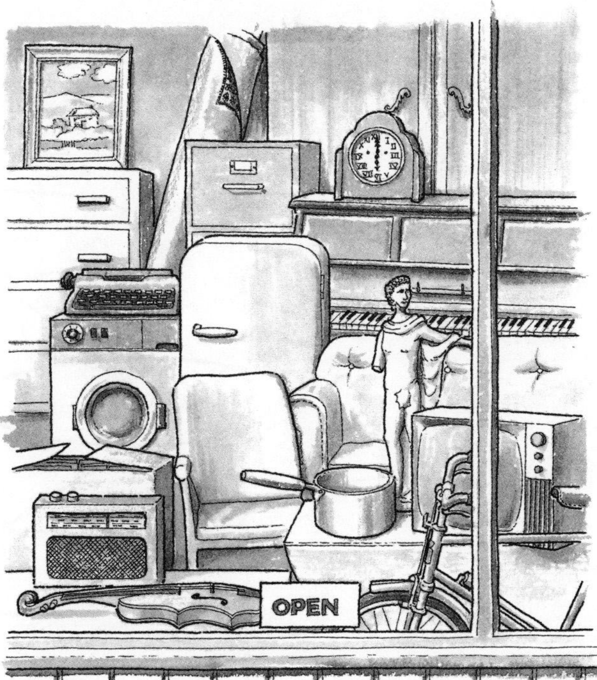

3 **Look at the picture, and then write ten sentences to say where things are. Examples:**

The fridge is between the sofa and the washing machine.
The clock is on the piano.

You will need these words.

bicycle chair clock filing-cabinet fridge piano picture radio saucepan sofa statue table TV typewriter violin washing machine

4 **Put in *there is, there are, there was, there were* or *there will be.***

1. .... a meeting of all heads of department at ten o'clock tomorrow morning.
2. .... two men at the door. They want to speak to you.
3. I got there late, and .... no more food.
4. I think .... a misunderstanding. Can I explain?
5. Were you working late? When I went past your house at two a.m. .... a light on.
6. In the village where I lived .... only about 50 people.
7. I think .... snow this evening or tonight.

5 **This is a 'vocabulary network'. Can you complete it with the words from the box?**

actors and actresses bank account bank manager film house policemen and policewomen shop stage

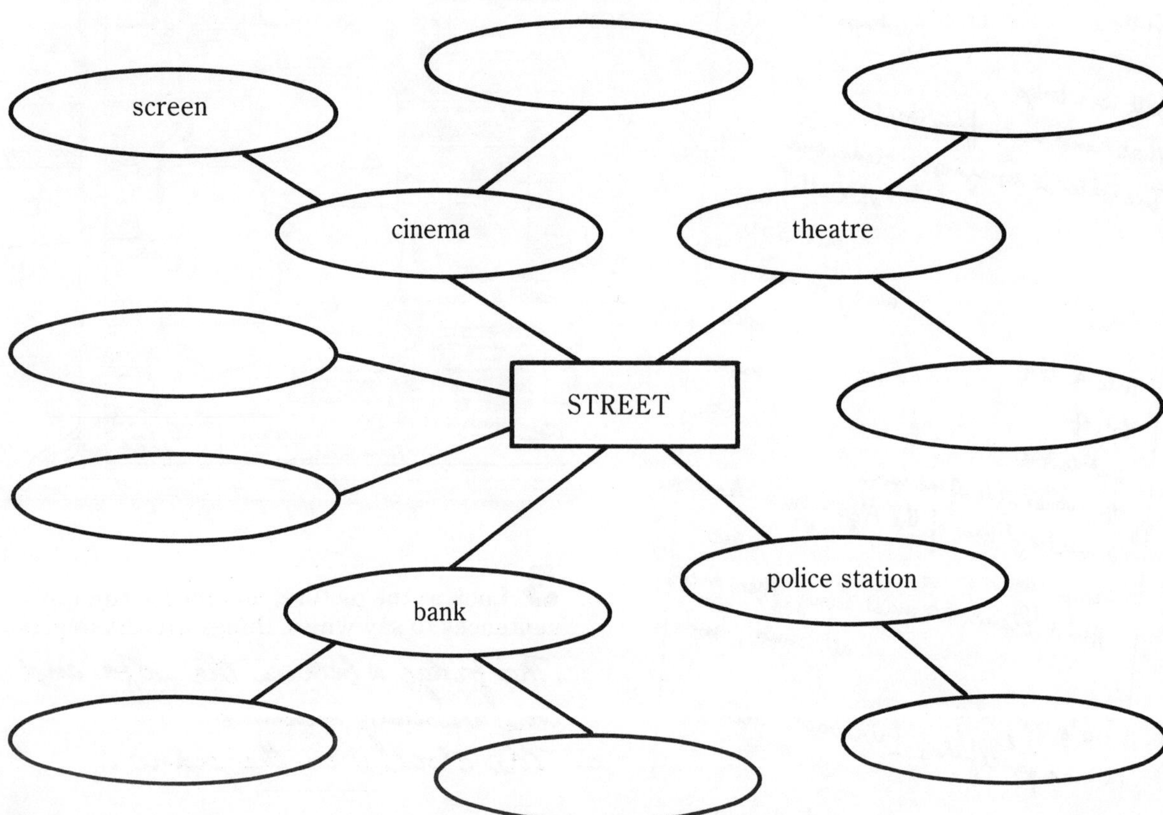

6 **Now can you make a vocabulary network starting with HOUSE? Here are some useful words; try to find some others, and make the network as big as you can. Use your dictionary to help you.**

bathroom ceiling chair door floor front door furniture roof room window

7 Strange but true. Read this with a dictionary.

One sixth of the earth's land surface is in the Soviet Union.

Nearly one eighth of the world's land surface is desert. Each day, the world's deserts increase by 160 sq km.

In Mammoth Caves National Park, in the United States, there is a cave system with nearly 300km of passages already explored.

In the Carlsbad Caverns, New Mexico, there is a cave 77 metres high and 550 metres across.

About 10% of the earth's land surface is covered with ice.

There is a place on the Antarctic continent where the land (under the ice cap) is 2,468 metres below sea level.

Greenland, the world's largest island (not counting Australia) is covered by a thick ice cap; there may in fact be a group of several islands underneath.

The coldest place in the world is Vostok, in Antarctica. Temperatures of −88° Centigrade have been recorded. (The world's hottest recorded temperature was 58°C at Al 'Aziziyah, in Libya.)

The largest iceberg ever seen was 335km long and 97km wide – larger than Belgium.

More than 70% of the earth's surface is covered by water.

The world's tallest mountain from base to summit is not Everest. It is Mauna Kea, on Hawaii, whose total height is 10,203 metres (including 5,998 metres below the surface of the sea).

The highest mountain which is completely below the surface of the sea is between Samoa and New Zealand – it is 8,690 metres high.

The world's longest rivers, the Amazon and the Nile, are both about 6,400km long from source to mouth.

The world's biggest lake is the Caspian Sea, between the Soviet Union and Iran.

The biggest lake in a lake is Manitou Lake (with an area of more than 100 sq km), on Manitoulin Island in Lake Huron, North America.

The world's highest waterfall is Angel Falls in Venezuela: the total drop is 979 metres.

B Things

1 What do they do? Use your dictionary and then write sentences.

A model		paints pictures.
A conductor		buys and sells works of art.
A composer		keeps financial records.
A housewife	is a	puts out fires.
A director	person	stops people parking in the wrong places.
A painter	who	leads an orchestra.
A builder		looks after a house and family.
A fireman		shows new clothes.
An art dealer		writes music.
An accountant		helps to run a company.
A traffic warden		builds houses.

....

....

....

....

....

....

....

....

....

....

....

2 Rewrite the sentences without *that* if possible. Examples:

I went and saw the film that you told me about.

I went and saw the film you told me about.

I've got a car that never breaks down.

I've got a car that never breaks down.

1. I've got some ear-rings that belonged to my grandmother.

   ....

2. I've finished the book that you lent me.

   ....

3. Here's the restaurant that you were talking about.

   ....

4. Do you know a word that means 'shut' and begins with *c*?

   ....

5. This is a letter that I forgot to give you yesterday.

   ....

6. They've got a lovely garden that runs down to a river.

   ....

7. Have you got a radio that I can borrow for a couple of hours?

   ....

3 Read the poem. Use a dictionary if necessary.

I like that stuff

Lovers lie around in it
Broken glass is found in it
Grass
I like that stuff

Tuna fish get trapped in it
Legs come wrapped in it
Nylon
I like that stuff

Eskimos and tramps chew it
Madame Tussaud gave status to it
Wax
I like that stuff

Elephants get sprayed with it
Scotch is made with it
Water
I like that stuff

Clergy are dumbfounded by it
Bones are surrounded by it
Flesh
I like that stuff

Harps are strung with it
Mattresses are sprung with it
Wire
I like that stuff

Carpenters make cots of it
Undertakers use lots of it
Wood
I like that stuff

Cigarettes are lit by it
Pensioners are happy when they sit by it
Fire
I like that stuff

Dankworth's alto is made of it, most of it,
Scoobedoo is composed of it
Plastic
I like that stuff

Man made fibres and raw materials
Old rolled gold and breakfast cereals
Platinum linoleum
I like that stuff

Skin on my hands
Hair on my head
Toenails on my feet
And linen on my bed

Well I like that stuff
Yes I like that stuff
The earth
Is made of earth
And I like that stuff

Adrian Mitchell

Madame Tussaud: the founder of a well-known museum in London which has wax models of famous people
clergy: priests
dumbfounded: astonished, very surprised
undertakers: people who organise funerals
Dankworth: a jazz musician
alto: kind of saxophone
scoobedoo: ornamental work in plastic

4 **Can you write one or more extra verses for the poem? (The words don't need to rhyme.)**

.... it
.... it
....
I like that stuff

.... it
.... it
....
I hate that stuff

.... it
.... it
....
I like that thing

.... it
.... it
....
I hate that thing

.... them
.... them
....
I like those things

.... them
.... them
....
I hate those things

5 **Put in the right prepositions.**

1. a chair: something you sit on
2. a picture: something you look ....
3. a radio: something you listen ....
4. a wardrobe: something you keep clothes ....
5. a bed: something you sleep ....
6. a table: something you put food ....

Families

A Different kinds of families

1 **Read the text, using your dictionary when necessary, and draw a line from each circled pronoun to the word it refers to. The first two are done for you.**

THE SWEDISH ANSWER: UNISEX MARRIAGE

BY SARA JOLLY

a British housewife who lived in Sweden for 3 years

WOULD you like a unisex marriage – with husband and wife sharing housework and breadwinning day and day about? I can only report that Swedish wives flourish on it. They are outward-looking, and a conversation with them is likely to be about their work, hobbies or families. It is scarcely ever about what so-and-so said to offend them, or what women's place in society ought to be.

They are enthusiastic in all kinds of ways. During the three years I lived in Sweden while my husband was working there, I repeatedly heard how much Swedish wives appreciated and enjoyed their families and homes because they were away from them for some of the time in their own careers.

The average Swede, though tall and handsome, doesn't spend much time paying a woman compliments. Perhaps this is because he is quite prepared to treat her as an equal.

When a young couple marry they don't take it for granted that the husband is the breadwinner, and the wife the housekeeper.

They have a flexible approach, sharing out the work and chores in a way which suits them. No one criticises them if they reverse their traditional roles.

As Katerina, a Swedish wife, explained to me: "Stefan and I have known each other since childhood. We went to the same kind of school, and we both trained as dentists, so why should only one of us have a career?"

A doctor who works in a Child Care Department thought that women had a right to work and to support themselves.

"I can understand a woman who prefers housework to factory work, but I just cannot understand an educated woman who doesn't work."

"When we married I was studying," a woman psychiatrist told me. "And, of course, when I qualified I started to practise." She could not imagine training and then not using her vital skills.

Nor is it only professional women who expect to work. The girl who came to clean my house told me that her husband was a postman.

"He's up early, and then he comes home early in the afternoon and looks after the baby while I go out to work."

Increasingly, the Swedish husband accepts that household chores are partly his responsibility.

(from *The Daily Telegraph*)

2 **Have families changed in your country or are they the same as they were a century ago? Write eight or more sentences about this. Try to use some of the words from this list.**

also although and because besides but so

....

....

....

....

....

....

3 Look at the family tree. Then use words from the box to complete the sentences.

Harry Webber = Mary Webber

Ronald Hunter = Ann Webber

Joseph Webber = Catherine Cook

Peter Hunter

Helen Webber

wife husband father mother brother sister son daughter aunt uncle niece nephew cousin grandfather grandmother grandson granddaughter brother-in-law sister-in-law father-in-law mother-in-law son-in-law daughter-in-law

1. Harry is Ann's ....
2. Mary is Joseph's ....
3. Harry is Mary's ....
4. Ann is Ronald's ....
5. Helen is Catherine's ....
6. Peter is Mary's ....
7. Joseph is Ann's ....
8. Helen is Harry's ....
9. Catherine is Harry's ....
10. Peter is Helen's ....
11. Catherine is Peter's ....
12. Mary is Ronald's ....

Now use the rest of the words from the box to write more sentences about the people in the family tree.

4 Revision. Match the beginnings and the ends of the definitions.

An American is	a place where you can watch films.
A match is	a person who comes from America.
A cinema is	a thing that you light a cigarette with.
A chair is	a piece of furniture for sitting on.
Breakfast is	getting from a lower place to a higher place.
Water is	a meal that you eat in the morning.
Climbing is	something you wash yourself in.

Now choose ten of these and write definitions for them.

a businessman	an office	a lighter
a guitar	juice	a cheque
a motorbike	paper	returning
a butcher	a key	ringing someone
hair	a passport	lunch
a neck	a campsite	a customer
a hat	sugar	tea
a neighbour	a canteen	a map
stealing	preferring	a dentist
a nose	a car	medicine
a cafe	a lorry	spelling
pepper	a cassette	a driver
a jacket	an ear	a mirror
refusing	a disco	milk

5 **Write a few sentences about someone in your family that you are proud of.**

6 **Revision. Invent the other half of this phone conversation.**

SHOP: Hello. Samuel's Jeweller's.

CUSTOMER: ....

SHOP: Did you drop it?

CUSTOMER: ....

SHOP: Well, we can have a look at it, but we're pretty busy right now. It'll take two weeks to repair.

CUSTOMER: ....

SHOP: Oh, in that case we can try to have it ready by then. Can you bring it in this afternoon?

CUSTOMER: ....

SHOP: Until five thirty.

CUSTOMER: ....

SHOP: All right, I'll see you then. Goodbye.

CUSTOMER: ....

B Family life

1 **Invent ends for these sentences.**

1. Parents should ....
2. Children should ....
3. Teachers should ....
4. Politicians should ....
5. Everybody should ....
6. I should ....

2 **Do you remember how to write plurals? Write the plurals of these words.**

boy ....
watch ....
lady ....
box ....
gun ....
day ....
church ....
potato ....
party ....
coach ....

way ....
lorry ....
reason ....
body ....
valley ....
switch ....
economy ....
tomato ....
difference ....

Do you remember the plurals of these words? Look them up in your dictionary if you are not sure.

child ....
person ....
woman ....
wife ....
knife ....
foot ....

3 Put punctuation and capital letters where they belong. The first ones are done for you as an example.

D K
~~d~~ear ~~k~~evin,

S
14 ~~s~~eptember 1985

im writing to ask you for some advice barbara and i are getting very worried about richard he has been staying out very late at night and is always too tired to do well in school last week he was out till one in the morning on tuesday and wednesday he wont listen to anything we say we have tried not giving him pocket money but it doesnt do any good i am afraid that now he is sure that we are just trying to make him do what we want to prove we are strong but the truth is we are worried about his future

i know you and simon had a rough patch when he was sixteen or so what did you do about it how did you handle it any advice you could give us would be very welcome we have run out of ideas ourselves

sorry to write such a short letter but i want to get this in the post today give my love to angela and the kids

yours

tony

4 Now imagine you are the son in Exercise 3, or the daughter in Exercise 6 in the Student's Book, and write a letter to a friend about your problems with your parents.

5 Revision.
A machine for drying hair is called a *hair dryer*. A thing for opening tins is called a *tin opener*. Write the words for:

a machine for playing records

....

a machine for mixing food

....

a thing that times eggs (when they're boiling)

....

things for warming people's legs

....

stuff that kills flies

....

a liquid that removes paint

....

a tool that opens bottles

....

a thing for peeling potatoes

....

a liquid for removing eye makeup

....

stuff for freshening the air

....

Hopes and wishes

A Would you like to have a white Rolls Royce?

1 Complete the text with the words and expressions in the box.

age	be able to	because	both	changed my mind	hope	idea	I've had	languages	less
like	medicine	never	round	speaking	still	thought	try to	wanted	wanted me	which

My parents .... to be a doctor, but I'm afraid I wasn't all that interested in .... More than anything else, I .... to travel – I thought I would .... to be a diplomat or a spy, I wasn't sure .... Foreign .... fascinated me, perhaps .... I was so bad at communicating in English and I .... a new language would give me another chance. So I decided that I was going to .... learn two languages a year; I saw myself .... 20 languages perfectly by the .... of 25. Full of enthusiasm, I started off with French and German. Somehow I .... got past those two, though I do speak them .... fairly well.

As time went on, the .... of being a diplomat or a spy became .... attractive. I .... and became a teacher. It's an interesting job, and I quite like it, but after 20 years .... about enough. I .... want to travel, and I .... that soon I may .... take a year off and go .... the world.

2 Write about your wishes and hopes, and how they have changed. Use some of the words and expressions from Exercise 1.

3 Add -s if necessary.

1. Andrew would like . –. to speak to you.
2. My mother want *s*. . to travel.
3. She can . . . speak five languages.
4. Our dog like . . . toast and marmalade.
5. The car need . . . oil.
6. Robert say . . . that he hope . . . you'll have time to see him.
7. I think . . . it may . . . rain.
8. Sally went . . . to Germany last year.
9. Everybody know . . . what's going to happen . . .

4 Read this letter. Then write a letter to Father Christmas (Santa Claus) asking for presents for yourself; or your family; or an organisation you belong to; or your country.

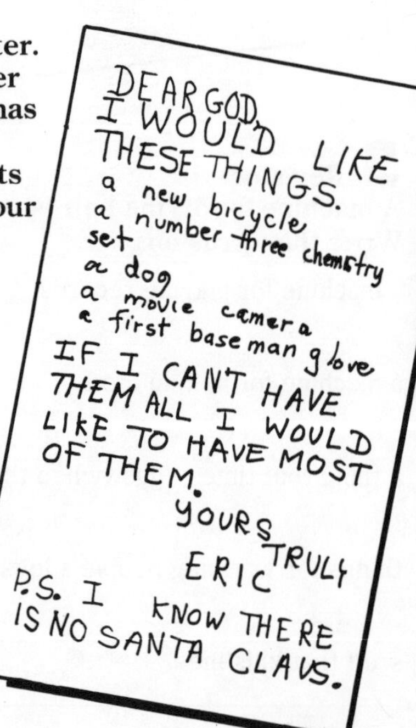
DEAR GOD,
I WOULD LIKE
THESE THINGS.
a new bicycle
a number three chemistry set
a dog
a movie camera
a first baseman glove
IF I CAN'T HAVE
THEM ALL I WOULD
LIKE TO HAVE MOST
OF THEM.
YOURS TRULY
ERIC
P.S. I KNOW THERE
IS NO SANTA CLAUS.

5 Revision. Complete these shopping dialogues with appropriate words and expressions.

1. SHOP ASSISTANT: Can I help you?
   CUSTOMER: Not just now, thank you. ....

2. SHOP ASSISTANT: Can I help you?
   CUSTOMER: Yes, ...
   SHOP ASSISTANT: What size?
   CUSTOMER: ....
   SHOP ASSISTANT: Here's a lovely one.
   CUSTOMER: ....
   SHOP ASSISTANT: £26.99.
   CUSTOMER: ....
   SHOP ASSISTANT: Of course. The changing rooms are just over here.

3. SHOP ASSISTANT: How do they fit, madam?
   CUSTOMER: ....
   SHOP ASSISTANT: No, not in that style. Would you like to see another similar style?
   CUSTOMER: ....

4. SHOP ASSISTANT: That will be £35.79, please.
   CUSTOMER: ....
   SHOP ASSISTANT: Yes, Access, Visa, Diner's Club and American Express.

6 Revision. Fill in the table of irregular verbs. Learn the ones you don't know.

PRESENT	PAST TENSE	PAST PARTICIPLE
know	knew	known
find	....	....
learn	....	....
lend	....	....
lose	....	....
meet	....	....
pay	....	....
read	....	....
sell	....	....
send	....	....
show	....	....
sing	....	....
sit	....	....
sleep	....	....

7 Put the sentences with the right cartoons. There is one sentence too many.

1. It was Charlie's last wish, that people should have fun visiting him.
2. All I want is a little more than I'll ever get.
3. First you don't want to come to the party – now you don't want to leave.
4. Why do you want her to walk and talk when you keep telling me to sit down and keep quiet?
5. Hello, George – remember you said that although I was going to marry Martin James you'd always be waiting for me if ever I should change my mind?
6. I hope your mother won't be angry.
7. Very good, chaps, now we'll try it from the plane.

B

C

D

E

IN MEMORY

CHARLES

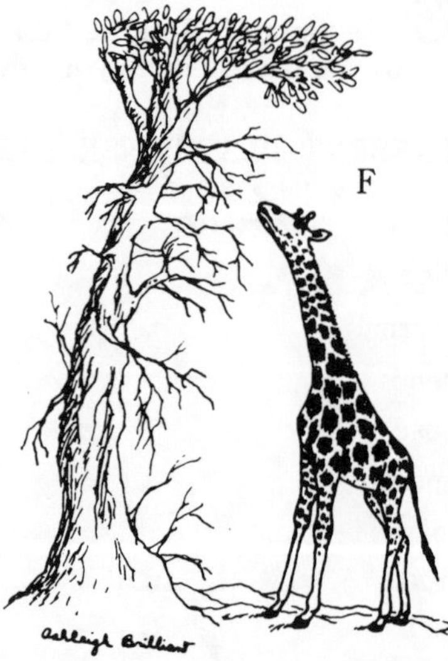

F

B Could you do me a favour?

1 Match the sentences on the left with the answers on the right.

Excuse me.	Sure. What is it?
Could you lend me £5?	That's all right.
Would you like to wait inside?	All right.
I've got a problem.	Not at all.
Thanks very much.	It's too expensive.
Could you do me a favour?	Thanks very much.
That's very kind of you.	Oh, yes? What's the matter?
Have you tried the Royal Hotel?	Yes?

2 Mark the stresses and then say the sentences.

1. Well, the thing is, I'm short of money.
2. That's very nice of you, John.
3. I'm sorry to trouble you.
4. Well, you see, it's like this.
5. We wondered if we could use your phone.
6. Would you like to have a look?

3 Revision. Make these sentences negative.

1. I can swim.
   I cannot (can't) swim.
2. I like walking.
   I do not (don't) like walking.
3. It is raining.
4. Mr Hancock lives here.
5. His grandparents speak Greek.
6. You will have a good day tomorrow.
7. Sally has got a cold.
8. That door should be closed.
9. The window was broken yesterday.
10. I'd like to live alone.
11. They want some help.
12. I waited till six o'clock.
13. She was pretty when she was a baby.

Unit 15B

4 **Study the advertisements and the letter (which answers one of the advertisements).**

Then choose one of the other advertisements and write a letter in answer to it.
(Note: s.a.e. = stamped addressed envelope.)

GUIDANCE FOR ALL AGES!
8-14 years: Advice for parents on schools, progress, IQ
15-24 years: Career Guidance, courses, finding work, changes
25-34 years: Career Development, promotion, improvements
35-54 years: Review, Redundancy, 2nd careers, new horizons
Whatever your age or decision, we can help. Free brochure:
CAREER ANALYSTS 90 Gloucester Pl. W1. 01-935 5452 (24hrs)

THE NATURAL BREAK
a conservation working holiday.
Spend a week looking after Britain's open spaces. No experience needed for drystone walling, hedging, footpath construction, etc. FREE brochure (A4 sae welcomed) from
Conservation Volunteers,
Room 1. 36 St Mary's St,
Wallingford, Oxon.
Tel. 0491 39766.

13 South Drive,
Norwich,
Norfolk NR4 6GK
17th July 1985

Dear Sirs,

I am interested in writing and selling children's stories. Would you please send me your free booklet? I enclose a stamped addressed envelope, and look forward to hearing from you.

Yours faithfully,

A. Dixon.

VISA TRAVEL
People you can trust and rely on
WORLD-WIDE TRAVEL

Amstrdm	£69	Paris	£60
K Lmpr	£375	Hongkg	£440
Singpre	£385	Cairo	£195
Jeddah	£320	Colmbo	£330
N York	£204	Joburg	£445
Nairobi	£310	Bombay	£325
Karachi	£265	T Aviv	£159
LA	£360	Toronto	£229
Tokyo	£530	Athens	£115

SYDNEY/MELB £555
01-437 1373/437 1216
35 Oxford Street, W1.
VISA TRAVEL VISA TRAVEL VISA TRAVEL VISA TRAVEL VISA TRAVEL VISA TRAVEL

WRITE & SELL children's stories. Mail tuition. Free booklet. Children's Features (O), 5-9 **Bexley Sq,** Salford, Manchester M3 6DB

YOUR BOOK PUBLISHED, and sold! Details: New Horizon (00), 25 Station Road, Bognor Regis

FREE CAREER BOOKLET
Train for success, for a better job, better pay
Enjoy all the advantages of an ICS Diploma Course, training you ready for a new, higher paid, more exciting career.
Learn in your own home, in your own time, at your own pace, through ICS home study, used by over 8 million already! Look at the wide range of opportunities awaiting you. Whatever your interest or skill, there's an ICS Diploma Course there for you to use.
Send for your FREE CAREER BOOKLET today-no cost or obligation at all.
ICS
ICS Dept NJS74
160 Stewarts Road
London SW8 4UJ

01-622 9911
(all hours)
CACC

5 Try the crossword.

(Solution on page 143.)

ACROSS

1. How big is .... moon?
6. I can't talk right now – I'm in a ....
8. My brother is an artist, but I can't .... a thing.
10. I can't carry this – it's .... heavy.
11. I'd like .... have a swimming pool.
14. I'd like to live to .... 100 years old.
15. I hope it won't .... too hot to have lunch in the garden.
18. It .... every day for 25 days last May; I hope the weather's better this year.
19. This helps you do a job.
20. There's one on the right side of your head.
21. I was .... home working in the garden when I heard the news.
22. Opposite of *wet.*
24. This has got four wheels.
26. Sister-in-............
27. Opposite of *light.*
30. Opposite of *before.*
31. Would you .... if I looked at your newspaper?
34. Your fairy .... might give you three wishes.
35. A chicken might come out of this.
37. Brother's son.
38. Come ....! How nice to see you!

DOWN

2. Please don't let the children play here – they might get ....
3. Have you .... your breakfast yet?
4. I .... a £5 note this morning, and I've only got 50p left now – where did it all go?
5. Past tense of *sit.*
7. Mine, ..., his, hers.
9. I .... if I could use your car this evening?
12. I .... fine earlier today, but now I've got a terrible headache.
13. Do you cook your eggs in butter or ....?
14. You can't get on a plane without a .... pass.
16. You have got one on the left side of your head.
17. I may not win this race, but I'm certainly going to ....
23. What's the ....? Have you hurt yourself?
25. Am, ..., is.
28. I'd like to .... and shave before we go to dinner.
29. 'How much does it cost?' 'It's ....'
31. 'Someone phoned.' 'A .... or a woman?'
32. Have you .... your homework?
33. You can sometimes see this in the sky at night.
36. You can kill someone with this.

Money

A Where does all the money go?

"This is no way to fight inflation, Saunders – I gave you a rise this morning."

1 Put one of these words or expressions in each blank. Use one word twice.

a lot	a lot of	enough	how much	less
more	much	too much		

1. I've spent .... money on books this month; I must spend less next month.
2. She earns .... than her sister, but she enjoys her job more.
3. We must go out .... this year: we spent far too much on theatre tickets and babysitting last year.
4. I spent .... on transport last year, but I think I will spend less now that I work closer to home.
5. I spent .... on my son's clothes than on my own last year – he was growing so fast.
6. I didn't spend .... on my holiday last year – I decided to spend more on my flat instead.
7. Don't put .... in that box or you won't be able to carry it.
8. .... is one Deutsche Mark in your currency?
9. Have you got .... or shall I give you some more?

2 Put the words in the right order.

1. to next money cinema I less must on month spend going the . I must spend less money on going to the cinema next month.
2. clothes year Sheila buy can more next . ...
3. give mother to must we more your money . ...
4. must to I week manager speak bank this my . ...
5. Robin show can your I budget to ? ....
6. abroad holiday can we this on year think I go . ...

3 Write a few lines about how you or your family spend your money. Do you think you spend too much or not enough on some things?

4 **Read this. You can look up the words marked * if you want, but *do not look up any other words in the dictionary* until you have answered the questions. Then you can look up other words if you want.**

An intriguing new book, *World paychecks: who makes what, where and why*, makes some fascinating international comparisons*. In Japan, for example, teachers earn far less than factory* workers, but in Denmark they are near the top of the wages scale. A New York dustman* makes three times as much as an Indian army general*. A German bus driver gets double the pay packet of a British bus driver. In China university professors* earn as much as government ministers, but Chinese journalists* are the most poorly paid ones in the world. And so on.

In part, says the writer, this reflects the law of supply* and demand*. New York dustmen are well paid because it is hard to find enough people who want to do the job, and in India generals do badly because everyone (well almost everyone) wants to be a general. But other facts – prestige*, passion, etc. – also make a difference.

It may interest you to know that the President of the United States earns three times what the Prime Minister of Britain does, but that the Prime Ministers of India and China get only about £40 a week. The best paid job in politics probably belongs to President Mobutu of poverty*–stricken Zaire, whose annual* earnings run into millions. I leave you to draw your own conclusion.

One of the other nuggets of information in the book is that Britain places a higher value* on its civil* servants* than America and most of Europe. Don't ask me who decides these things; no one asked for *my* opinion.

(from an article by William Davis in *Punch*)

1. True or false: in Denmark, factory workers earn more than teachers.
2. Who earns more, an Indian army general or a New York dustman?
3. If a British bus driver earns £500 a month, how much does a German bus driver earn?
4. Who earns more in China, university professors or journalists?
5. Which is true:
   A lot of people want to be New York dustmen.
   Not many people want to be New York dustmen.
6. Who earns more, the President of the United States or the President of Zaire?
7. Do civil servants earn more in America or in Britain?

5 **Vocabulary revision. Circle the word that is different in each list.**

1. behind since by above
2. all both some always
3. east age sex weight
4. angry glad pretty worried
5. open ask tell say
6. bag box glass book
7. century yard hour second
8. run walk kiss jump

(Answers on page 143.)

6 **Grammar revision. Fill in the blanks in the table.**

I	me	my	mine
…………	…………	…………	…………
he	…………	…………	…………
she	…………	her	…………
it	…………	…………	…………
…………	us	…………	…………
they	…………	…………	…………

"Just your credit cards if you don't mind, sir – I don't feel safe on the streets with cash these days."

"Excuse me, sir, about that rise you promised me . . ."

Unit 16B

B I'll give you £25 for it

1 Put in *too much, too many* or (*not*) *enough.*

1. We've spent .... on alcohol this month. We *must* drink less whisky.
2. It's not really worth keeping the shop open – we aren't doing .... business.
3. You've really got .... cats – you should give some of them away.
4. I don't even want to read the newspaper any more. It's too depressing, there's .... bad news.
5. I've had .... bad luck in my life; I think it's time for some good luck.
6. I've done .... favours for her; she thinks I should do everything for her now.
7. He tells .... jokes; he should be more serious.
8. Don't worry – there are .... jobs to keep everybody busy.
9. We haven't had .... news about the accident to know whether it's really serious or not.
10. His books are far too serious for me; there's .... humour in them.

2 Think of a time in your life when you had too much, too many, or not enough of something. Write five or more sentences about what happened.

....

....

....

....

....

....

....

....

3 Complete the sentences with *too... to* or (*not*)*... enough to.* You can use the words in the box if you like.

calm	depressed	intelligent	old
strong	tall	tired	worried	young

1. *I thought she was too intelligent to* make a stupid mistake like that.
2. .... be President/Prime Minister.
3. .... drive a big lorry.
4. .... play football.
5. .... have a lot of children.
6. .... have grandchildren.
7. .... go to a party.
8. .... carry that box.
9. .... be a policeman/policewoman.
10. .... have a driving licence.
11. .... continue working now.

4 Fill the blanks in this dialogue with words and expressions from the lesson.

A: Why don't you come to the mountains with me next weekend?

B: Oh, I'd love to, but I've got far too much work to finish, and a .... is coming on Sunday evening.

A: Oh, come .... You can bring some of your work with you. And we can be back on Sunday in time for your friend. .... I'll pick you up at work on Friday afternoon and we can leave straight from there.

B: That sounds lovely. To ...., I've been dying for a weekend in the mountains. But I will bring some work along to do, ...

A: Great! I should tell you that the house is not in the best .... I can't .... to pay anyone to work on it, so I've been doing some decorating myself. One of the rooms is full of paint-brushes and ladders.

B: Oh, I don't mind that. Listen, this sounds lovely. Shall I bring some food along?

A: Great idea. See you on Friday at five, then?

B: Friday at five. And thanks again. Bye.

A: Bye.

5 Grammar revision. Change these sentences as in the examples.

I'll get a drink for you.

I'll get you a drink.

Sally bought a new shirt for me.

Sally bought me a new shirt.

1. Would you like me to make a sweater for you?

....

....

2. Shall I play some music for you?

....

3. Alice didn't show the letter to her mother.

....

4. I'm going to make a cake for everybody tomorrow.

....

5. We should send some money to David.

....

6. If you go to the shops, can you buy some stamps for Mary?

....

7. Next Christmas I'm going to get a table lamp for Kate and a toaster for Ruth.

....

....

6 **Put in prepositions where they are necessary. Sometimes no preposition is needed.**

I was walking to the shop ...—... yesterday when for some reason I thought about the day my son was born. He was born ...*on*... a windy morning .... June. We drove to the hospital .... ten o'clock the night before, and the wind was already strong. Branches were being blown from the trees; .... the time we got to the hospital we heard on the radio that the police were advising people not to go out unless it was necessary. It seemed strange for the wind to blow so hard without any rain. It just blew and blew .... twelve hours. And what seemed very strange to us was that it stopped almost as soon as my son was born: it blew very hard .... eight o'clock at night .... eight o'clock in the morning, and then just stopped.

I simply must do something about this garden .... next year. It's too late now to do much .... this year, though I suppose I could put a few bulbs in to have tulips and daffodils .... the spring. And then, ... March or so when the weather starts getting better, I'll start digging up the place and planting a few seeds. It's just that I've only been in this house .... February, you see, and I've never had a garden before. I don't really know much about gardening. But I plan to be here .... several years, at least, so I suppose I shall learn.

Unit 17

Before and after

A Do you get up as soon as you wake up?

1 **Look at the examples and then join the sentences together in the same way.**

I have breakfast. Then I get dressed.

I have breakfast before *I get dressed.*

I go to bed. Then I read for a bit.

I read for a bit after *I go to bed.*

1. I brush my teeth. Then I undress.
   .... before ....
2. I get into bed. Then I put the light out.
   .... after ....
3. I wake up. Then I get up at once.
   .... as soon as ....

4. I met Jane. Then my life changed.
 .... after ....
5. She was very unhappy. Then she left school.
 .... until ....
6. I thought I was very ill. Then I went to see the doctor.
 .... before ....
7. I telephoned Kate. Then I went to see her.
 .... before ....
8. I went to America. Then everything got better.
 .... after ....

2 Which happened first?

1. Before I went to France, I studied French for six months.
 First I studied French.
 Then I went to France.
2. After I left school, I made a lot of new friends.
 ....
 ....
3. Before I went out, I cleaned my shoes.
 ....
 ....
4. After you came to see me, I felt fine.
 ....
 ....
5. Before Andrew got to London, it started raining.
 ....
 ....
6. After it got dark, Paul went out for a walk.
 ....
 ....
7. Before I took off the handbrake, I looked in the mirror.
 ....
 ....
8. Just after your mother telephoned, your father came to see me.
 ....
 ....

3 Put in *still, yet* or *already.*

1. 'Haven't you finished ....?'
2. 'No, I'm .... working.'
3. 'When's Mary coming?' 'She's .... here.'
4. 'Are you ready?' 'No, I haven't done my packing ....'
5. Ann's doing very well at school. She's .... got three O Levels, and she's only 15.
6. 'What's the weather like?' 'It's .... raining.'
7. 'Is it lunchtime?' 'Not ....'
8. 'Have you phoned Godfrey ....?' 'No, I'm going to do it this evening.'
9. Look at the time! It's .... eight o'clock. We really must go.

"Let's get this straight, Simpson – after you had a bath, which plug did you pull out?"

4 Put in *So do I, So am I, So have I* etc. or *Neither do I, Neither am I, Neither can I* etc.

1. 'I think she's wrong.' '.............................'
2. 'Luke isn't going to come to work tomorrow.'
   '.............................'
3. 'I've had more than enough of this.'
   '.............................'
4. 'I can speak a bit of Chinese.'
   '.............................'
5. 'I'll be in London tomorrow.'
   '.............................'
6. 'I didn't come to school last week.'
   '.............................'
7. 'I wasn't very impressed by Patrick's ideas.'
   '.............................'
8. 'Alice wants them to change all their plans.'
   '.............................'

5 Put in *such* or *so*.

1. His letter was .... rude that I didn't know how to answer.
2. Ann's friends are .... strange!
3. I didn't know you had .... a big house.
4. I'm .... tired that I think I'm going to bed.
5. It was .... a slow train that it would have been faster to walk.
6. I've never met .... kind people as your family.
7. I didn't expect it to be .... cold – I wish I'd brought my coat.
8. It's been .... terrible weather that the farmers haven't been able to grow anything.

6 Can you fill in the gaps? Use some of the words in the box.

afraid again back borrow but can could couple course discuss few got how I am in lend letter listen message moment out speak speaking thanks that thinking this well who

ANN: Hello. Bristol 816547.

JOE: Hello. .... I .... to Ann, please?

ANN: .... Who's ....?

JOE: Oh, hello, Ann. .... is Joe. .... are you?

ANN: Fine, ... And you?

JOE: I'm OK. ...., Ann, I've .... a problem. I need a video recorder for a .... of days. Could you possibly .... me yours?

ANN: ...., I'll have to ask Phil. I'm .... he's not in at the .... Can I ring you ....?

JOE: Yes, of .... If I'm not ...., you can always leave a ....with Sally.

ANN: OK, Joe. I'll ring you as soon as I know.

JOE: Thanks a lot, Ann. Bye.

ANN: Bye.

"Good morning. Now that was what I call a real party."

7 See how much of this story you can understand *without* using a dictionary.

The Little Girl and the Wolf

One afternoon a big wolf waited in a dark forest for a little girl to come along carrying a basket of food to her grandmother. Finally a little girl did come along and she was carrying a basket of food. "Are you carrying that basket to your grandmother?" asked the wolf. The little girl said yes, she was. So the wolf asked her where her grandmother lived and the little girl told him and he disappeared into the wood.

When the little girl opened the door of her grandmother's house she saw that there was somebody in bed with a nightcap and nightgown on. She had approached no nearer than twenty-five feet from the bed when she saw that it was not her grandmother but the wolf, for even in a nightcap a wolf does not look any more like your grandmother than the Metro-Goldwyn lion looks like Calvin Coolidge. So the little girl took an automatic out of her basket and shot the wolf dead.

Moral: It is not so easy to fool little girls nowadays as it used to be.

(from *The Thurber Carnival*)

I hadn't seen her for a very long time

1 **Read the text (use a dictionary for the most difficult words). Some of the words have been blacked out: you will find them in the box. Write the correct word beside each blank.**

and	but	had	has	have
shall	was	were		

CRAZY BANK MACHINE PAYS £195 JACKPOT

Police █████ last night investigating the mystery of a mad money machine which handed out a jackpot payment to a weekend shopper. ....

Brewery worker Mr David Baker tapped out a request for £15 on a National Westminster Bank cash dispenser at Kingston, Surrey, and █████ rewarded with about £195 in crisp fivers. ....

At their home in Kingston his wife, Mrs Deborah Baker, 30, said: 'He immediately handed the money over to the police. He █████ quite astonished. ....

'Some of the money obviously belonged to the lady who █████ used the machine before him. She █████ wanted £50 and got nothing. ....

'The machine █████ obviously gone up the wall. My husband handed over the £50 to the lady behind him, █████ he was still left with quite a lot of money.' ....

A spokesman for National Westminster said: 'Luckily there █████ a member of the staff nearby █████ the machine █████ switched off. ....

'I just do not know what made it go berserk. It is a normally reliable machine. We █████ make a thorough investigation.' ....

At Kingston police station a spokesman said: 'We have had a number of complaints about the machine. I sent a special constable down to investigate but I █████ not heard from him for some time – perhaps he █████ gone to the South of France . . . ' ....

(*Sunday Express*)

2 **Imagine that you are David Baker. Write the story of what happened to you when you went to get money from the National Westminster Bank cash dispenser.**

3 **Can you complete the list of cardinal and ordinal numbers?**

1	*one*	*first*
2	......	......
3	......	......
4	......	......
5	......	......
6	......	......
7	......	......
8	......	......
9	......	......
10	......	......
11	......	......
12	......	......
13	......	......
14	......	......
15	......	......
16	......	......
17	......	......
18	......	......
19	......	......
20	......	......
21	......	......
30	......	......
100	......	......
1,000	......	......

4 **Can you pronounce these words with the right stress?**

someone directions goodbye recognition silence family realise suitcase restaurant reserve examine minute cinema language difficult afternoon repair

5 **Can you write the past tense and past participle of these verbs?**

INFINITIVE	PAST TENSE	PAST PARTICIPLE
become	*became*	*become*
break	......	......
bring	......	......
get	......	......
grow	......	......
hear	......	......
hold	......	......
lie	......	......
run	......	......
sing	......	......
sit	......	......
stand	......	......
take	......	......
wake	......	......

6 **Can you complete the list?**

January, February, ...

......

......

......

7 **Do you know the days of the week?**

What is the day after Thursday? ......

What is the day before the day before Tuesday?

......

What is the day after the day before Sunday?

......

What is today? ......

What was the day before yesterday?

......

What is the day after tomorrow?

......

What day is your birthday on this year?

......

Facts and opinions

A They thought the sun went round the earth

1 Complete the two texts with the past tenses of the verbs in the boxes. You can use a dictionary.

be be be eaten be made breathe come cry fall make

The Sulaco Indians believed that the sun and the moon .... brother and sister. The sun .... of gold, and the moon of silver. The Sulacos thought that the sun .... by a great bird every night. In the morning, just before dawn, the bird laid an egg and the sun .... out again.

When the sun .... angry, he .... fire and smoke: his breath .... the wind, the smoke was the storm-clouds and the fire was lightning. Mother sky (according to the Sulacos) was unhappy because her child the sun was angry. She ...., and her tears .... as rain.

be believe calculate go know last move move publish say show

The ancient Greeks .... that the world .... round, and they .... its size very accurately as early as 200 BC. But they .... that the earth was the centre of the universe, and that the sun and the planets .... round it. This belief .... until the 16th century, when Copernicus, a Polish astronomer, ... his book on the movements of the sun, moon, stars and planets. Copernicus .... that the earth and the planets .... in circles round the sun. Later, Kepler .... that the planets .... in ellipses, not circles.

2 Rewrite these sentences in 'reported speech'.

1. She asked me 'What is your name?' *She asked me what my name was.*
2. She asked me 'What do you want?' ....
3. She asked me 'Where do you live?' ....
4. I asked her 'Why do you want to know?' ....
5. She asked me 'Why don't you answer my questions?' ....
6. I asked her 'Is your father at home?' ....
7. She asked me 'Are you a friend of his?' ....
8. I asked her 'Do you remember me?' ....
9. She asked me 'Do you know what day it is?' ....
10. I asked myself 'What is she talking about?' ....

3 Read two or more of these texts, and say whether the sentences are true or false.

An absurd fiction of history is that when Columbus said the world was round, everybody else thought it was flat. During the debates at the court of Queen Isabella, the true shape of the Earth was never an issue; its size was! The opponents of Columbus said he was underestimating the size, and that he could never sail due west from Europe to the Orient. They were right. Except for the accident of an unknown continent in between, Columbus would either have turned back or been lost at sea.

1. At the court of Queen Isabella, people argued about how big the earth was. True.
2. When Columbus said the world was round, everybody else thought it was flat. ....
3. Columbus did not realise how big the earth was. ....

Until the time of Galileo, an argument used with potent effect was that if the Earth moved, and if it indeed rotated on its axis, the birds would be blown away, clouds would be left behind, and buildings would tumble.

4. Galileo argued that if the earth moved, buildings would fall down. ....

"The doctrine that the Earth is neither the center of the universe nor immovable, but moves, even with a daily rotation, is absurd, and both philosophically and theologically false, and at the least an error of Faith." This was the wording of the Roman Congregation's decision against Galileo.

5. The Roman Congregation said that the earth was the centre of the universe. ....

In and around Zion, a little town in Illinois, on the shore of Lake Michigan about forty miles north of Chicago, there are hundreds, perhaps thousands, of people who believe the Earth is not round. They are the supporters of a theory, proposed in the early 1900s by Wilbur Glenn Voliva, that the Earth is flat. There are also people today who believe the world is hollow and open at the poles. There are some who even believe the Earth is on the inside of a hollow sphere.

6. Some people in the United States believe that the earth is flat. ....

(from *The Book of Facts, II*, by Isaac Asimov)

4 Put the words with the right pictures.

hard	heavy	light	long	rough	round
short	smooth	soft	square	thick	thin

....

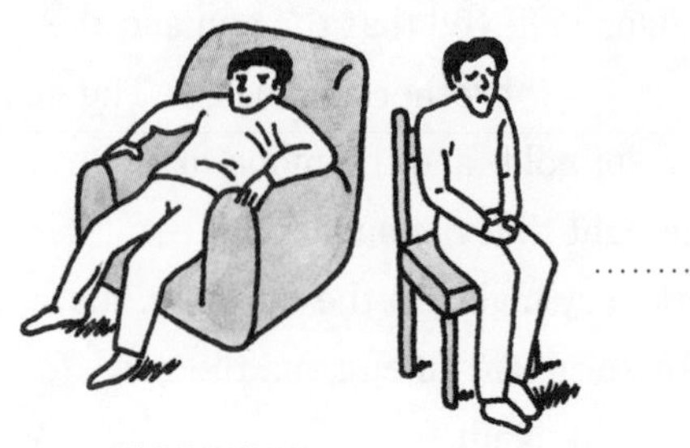

....

....

....

....

B Probability

1 Put in *will, might, can't* or *must.*

1. Next Monday .... be my 30th birthday.
2. I .... go to Spain next week, but I don't think it's very likely.
3. 'Isn't that Joan over there?' 'No, it .... be her – Joan's much taller than that.'
4. There's somebody at the door. Do you think it .... be the postman?
5. 'I've been travelling since four o'clock.' 'You .... be tired.'
6. We haven't made definite plans for our holiday yet. We .... go to Greece or Italy, or we .... even stay at home.
7. This .... be John's coat. There's a letter addressed to him in the pocket.
8. 'I'm getting married next week.' 'You .... mean it!' 'I do.'

2 Make some sentences (at least six).

I'm likely
I'm not likely
. . . is likely
. . . is not likely

to get rich.
to live to be 90.
to go to the United States next year.
to fall in love soon.
to become President.
to get a gold medal in the next Olympics.
to speak good English one day.
to travel a lot next year.
to get a letter tomorrow.
to . . .

....

....

....

....

....

....

....

....

....

....

....

....

....

....

....

....

3 Look at the table of prices for the last four years. Can you predict next year's prices?

Example:

A dictionary is likely to cost about £3.40.
(OR: between £3.30 and £3.50.)

	3 YEARS AGO	2 YEARS AGO	LAST YEAR	THIS YEAR
Greek-English dictionary	£1.85	£2.10	£2.50	£2.90
Fordwagen car	£3,500	£3,900	£4,350	£4,650
Welsh blue cheese (1lb)	£0.60	£0.80	£1.10	£1.35
JLX76 calculator	£35	£25	£18	£12.50
Fish & chips	£0.80	£0.95	£1.20	£1.45

Predict the prices of some things in your country next year.

4 Two problems.

1. You are trying to win money at roulette, by betting on red or black. Red has come up the last ten times. How do you think you should bet?
   A. Red is more likely to come up, so you should bet on red.
   B. Black is very likely to come up next time, so you should bet on black.
   C. Red and black are equally likely, so it doesn't matter how you bet.
2. A couple have four children. What are the chances that they have two boys and two girls?
   A. 50–50. B. More than 50–50.
   C. Less than 50–50.
   (Answers on page 143.)

5 Read this with a dictionary.

In 1898, an American author named Morgan Robertson, who wrote his novels in a trancelike state of consciousness, published *The Wreck of the Titan*, a book that describes the tragic maiden voyage of the largest luxury liner ever built, the unsinkable *Titan*. Seventy-five thousand tons dead-weight, she had three propellers, a top speed of twenty-five knots, and carried 2,000–3,000 passengers. But she only had twenty-four lifeboats, far too few to accommodate all the passengers, and on a foggy night in April she crashed into, and was sunk by, a massive iceberg.

The *Titanic* was built thirteen years later; she also displaced 75,000 tons, had three screws and a maximum speed of twenty-five knots. She was "the largest craft afloat" and had the same reputation for invulnerability. On her maiden voyage in 1912, the *Titanic* sank after encountering an iceberg on the night of April 14, in thick fog. There were 2,207 passengers on board, but only twenty lifeboats; fifteen hundred people died.

(from *Curious Facts* by John May)

6 Try the crossword.

(Solution on page 143.)

ACROSS

1. More than one child.
5. The opposite of *yes*.
6. I look like .... father.
7. A heavy weight.
11. Part of your body at the top of your leg.
13. Galileo said that the earth goes .... the sun.
14. 'I'm sorry.' 'That's .... right.'
15. You'd better pick that glass up, ... somebody will break it.
16. I beg your ....?
19. I didn't do it .... purpose.
20. A person who specialises in one of the sciences.

DOWN

1. You take photos with it.
2. Not out.
3. Many.
4. The past of *run*.
8. Not young.
9. Petrol is made from it.
10. People thought the planets moved in circles, ... in fact they moved in ellipses.
11. It's .... work learning a language.
12. The Earth is one; so is Mars.
15. The same as *15 across*.
16. An American writer: Edgar Allen ....
17. A woman's first name.
18. You're not quite as tall .... me, are you?

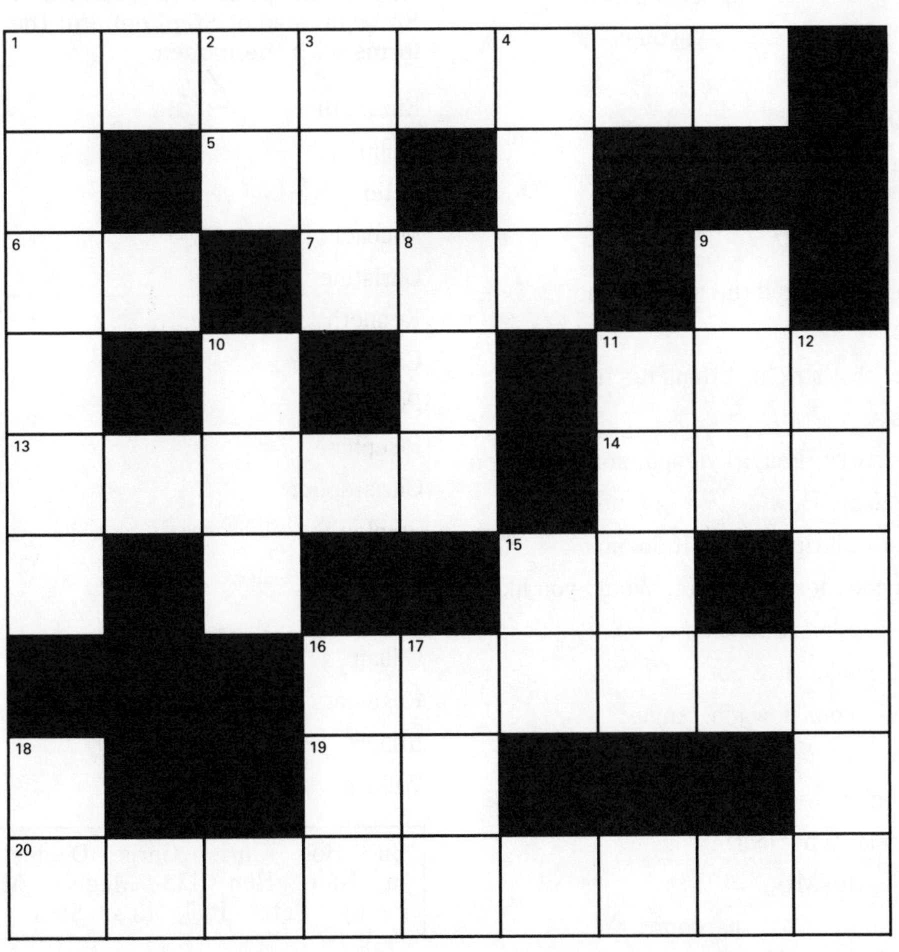

Unit 1

Small talk

A Hello, nice to see you

1 **Try to complete the conversation. Then look at Dialogues 1–3 (Student's Book page 157), and check your answers.**

POLLY: There's the doorbell.

JAKE: .... go.
(Jake opens the door.)
Hello, Angela. Hello, Ted. .... to see you.

ANGELA: Hello, Jake. It's been a long time. Who .... is coming?

JAKE: Pete and Liz. Come on in. .... take your coat.

POLLY: Hello. I'm so .... you could come.

JAKE: What .... I .... you to drink?

ANGELA: .... a gin and tonic.

TED: So .... I.

ANGELA: You've changed the room round, ... you?

POLLY: Yes, that's right. I think it's nicer like this.

TED: Oh, sorry, Polly. I've spilt some tonic on the floor. How .... of me.

POLLY: That's all right, Ted. It doesn't ....

JAKE: It's good for the carpet. Would you like .... more tonic?

TED: No, thanks. I've got ....

JAKE: How's your new job, Angie?

ANGELA: Nice, but very .... work.

POLLY: I didn't know you'd got a new job, Angela. What is it?

ANGELA: PA to the MD.

POLLY: .... pardon?

ANGELA: Personal Assistant to the Managing Director.

POLLY: Well, that .... be interesting.

ANGELA: .... depends. The work's interesting, but the MD's ....

POLLY: Oh, dear. That's a pity.

JAKE: How's your glass? .... another drink.

2 **People's families and friends often use short forms of their first names (for example, *Steve* instead of *Stephen*). Put the right short forms with the names.**

Elizabeth ....Liz....
Philip ....
Peter ....
Michael ....
Christine ....
Kenneth ....
Catherine ....
Penelope ....
Josephine ....
Christopher ....
Stanley ....
Margaret ....
Deborah ....
Gillian ....
Rosemary ....
Robert ....
William ....

Bill	Bob	Chris	Chris	Debbie	Gill
Jo	Kate	Ken	Liz	Maggie	Mike
Penny	Pete	Phil	Ros	Stan	

3 Revision. Put in the correct preposition.

1. I like listening .... music in the evenings.
2. We spent yesterday evening looking .... my mother's old photos.
3. Excuse me. I'm looking .... a good dictionary. Have you got one?
4. Could I speak .... the manager, please?
5. I've been living here .... six years.
6. We were talking .... politics.
7. I'd like a book .... a six-year-old child, please.
8. We're going on holiday .... Ann and Pete this year.

4 Here are some answers. What are the questions?

1. I was talking to my sister.
   Who were you talking to?
2. The letter's from the bank.
   ....
3. I'm thinking about my girlfriend.
   ....
4. I had lunch with Carola and Sue.
   ....
5. I think she's looking at a bird in the garden.
   ....
6. It was written by my teacher.
   ....
7. I got it from Charlie.
   ....
8. I'm talking about the demonstration.
   ....

5 Write the question-tags.

1. She's very beautiful, *isn't she?*
2. You live in Birmingham, ...
3. It was a lovely meal, ...
4. You've been to Greece already,
   ....
5. We'll be late, ...
6. You're coming with us, ...
7. It's really hot today, ...
8. Simon came the same year as you,
   ....
9. Bob's left school, ...

"Did they lose?"

6 Guessing words from context. Here is a part of a letter from Martha to a friend, about a dinner-party conversation. Read it without a dictionary, and then try and do the exercise.

The occasion was a dinner party given at the house of Nigel, a colleague of Josh, to show his collection of Top People and put up with a few Bottom People like me.

At the dining table I was seated next to a gentleman in a blazer with a very hostile moustache. During the next thirty minutes, through soup, salmon, peas and potatoes, he told me about sparking plugs. By the time the strawberries arrived, I knew more about sparking plugs than whoever invented sparking plugs and, at the advent of the cheese board, I decided to defend myself. I started telling him about the baby. I told him all I know about the baby, what the baby eats and what the baby refuses to eat. I talked at length about the baby's little ways. I was very animated about the baby; he was strangely quiet. As the brandy was poured, he turned to the woman on his left and left me alone, at last, with my Remy Martin.

And, believe it or not, Josh noticed and Josh minded. 'What happened to you?' he asked when we got home. 'Don't you realise that men at parties are not interested in hearing about babies? Haven't you learned that babies are hardly the ideal coin of conversational currency?' 'That I have, Josh,' I said. 'I understand that fact perfectly. When a man's eyes go blank, when he stares at my right ear, when he fidgets like someone with itching powder in his pants, Martha gets the message. And what do I care, says Martha. Does man realise when woman is bored? He does not. He refuses even to imagine that sparking plugs are not everyone's favourite thing. "Fair is fair," I said to that man, "do you have children?" "Yes," he said. "Well, I don't have sparking plugs so I win." 'Why, oh husband, is it shameful of me to bore a man to death at a party by talking babies, and all right for him to bore me to death talking of sparking plugs?' 'Martha,' said Josh, 'you've had too much to drink.' 'Possibly, Josh,' I said. 'There is, I agree, a remote possibility,' and then I fell down.

(from *Letters from a Fainthearted Feminist* by Jill Tweedie – adapted)

Match each word in column A with the meaning in column B that suits it best. Be careful: there are too many meanings in column B.

A	B
1. blazer (line 6)	a. looks hard
2. advent (line 11)	b. habits
3. ways (line 15)	c. chair
4. animated (line 15)	d. small chance
5. at last (line 18)	e. finally
6. stares (line 26)	f. end
7. fidgets (line 26)	g. jacket
8. shameful (line 34)	h. friends
9. remote possibility (line 38)	i. full of life
	j. moves about
	k. talks
	l. arrival
	m. very bad

B I didn't think much of it

1 **Write the names of books you have read, films you have seen, etc. After each one, write what you thought of it. Use some of the expressions from the box. Example:**

Supergirl: I didn't think much of it.

....

....

....

....

....

....

....

I thought it was great. I liked it very much.
I really liked it. I didn't think much of it.
It didn't say anything to me.
I didn't like it. I didn't like it at all.
Complete rubbish. It made me laugh.
It made me cry. It made me sick.
I thought it was boring.

2 **Put in *So do I, So am I, So have I,* etc; or *Neither do I, Neither am I, Neither have I,* etc.**

1. 'I like watching tennis.' '*So do I.*'
2. 'I'm not hungry.' '*Neither am I.*'
3. 'I'll come back tomorrow.' '..................................'
4. 'I've got a cold.' '..................................'
5. 'I can't understand a word he says.' '..................................'
6. 'I've never been to Africa.' '..................................'
7. 'I enjoyed the party.' '..................................'
8. 'I don't think much of her new boyfriend.' '..................................'
9. 'I thought it was complete nonsense.' '..................................'
10. 'I was bored the whole time.' '..................................'
11. 'I didn't like it at all.' '..................................'
12. 'I'll be glad when today's finished.' '..................................'
13. 'I'm not thirsty.' '..................................'
14. 'I'm very tired.' '..................................'

3 **Try to complete these sentences. Then look at Dialogue 5 (Student's Book page 158) and check your answers.**

1. We've got a long way ....
2. We .... to be .... our way.
3. We'd .... be going.
4. Thank you .... coming.
5. You .... come over to us soon.

4 **Disagree.**

1. It wasn't like that at all.
   Yes, it was.
2. She's been there twice.
   No, she hasn't.
3. They came at Christmas.
   ....
4. I wasn't here that day.
   ....
5. She isn't very clever.
   ....
6. John's left his job.
   ....
7. They don't live in London.
   ....
8. I was here first.
   ....
9. We'll be on time.
   ....
10. He's going to fall.
    ....
11. They weren't any good.
    ....
12. Anna can't swim.
    ....
13. Lorna didn't come early.
    ....
14. Jack's got a new car.
    ....

5 **Read the thank-you letter.**
Now choose one of these situations and write a thank-you letter.

1. You have spent a week with a friend at the seaside home of his/her parents. They have been very kind to you, lent you their boat, etc. Write a thank-you letter to the parents.
2. You (and your husband/wife/boyfriend/girlfriend/family) have been to Sunday lunch at your best friend's home, and have met his/her fiancé(e) for the first time. Write a thank-you letter and invite them back for a meal.
3. You have been taken to lunch by an old friend of your father's/mother's who was in your town for the day. Write, thanking him/her for the meal.
4. You have just moved to a new town/city and someone who works with you has had you to dinner at his/her home. You have discovered that you both like opera (or jogging or stamp-collecting or something else). Write a thank-you letter and suggest that you do something together. Make a specific suggestion.

6 August 1985

Dear Sarah,

Just a note to say thank you for the lovely day yesterday. It was really hard to get back to work today after such a relaxing time. Delicious food, good company, a beautiful garden – it really felt like a mini-holiday. The kids had a great time too, and are still talking about the dog and the pool. It was especially nice to meet your parents after hearing about them for so long; they really are just as I imagined them.

Would you like to come over to us next weekend? You could come for lunch on Saturday or Sunday, and we could go for a walk in the hills afterwards if the weather is good. Please bring your parents if they are still staying with you. It would be lovely to see them again.

Hoping to see you next weekend, and with thanks again for yesterday,

Love,

Kate

6 Complete the lists.

1. I, ...
2. me, ...
3. my, ...
4. mine, ...
5. myself, ...

....

7 How do you spell the past tense forms of these verbs?

work	take	change ....
play	beg	stop ....
move	touch	cry ....

Unit 20

Do it

A How to do it

1 Complete these sentences with the words from the box.

by can if to

1. You .... save petrol .... not driving at over 55mph.
2. .... make stale bread taste fresh, dip it in cold water and heat it.
3. .... shoe polish gets hard, warm it for a few minutes.
4. You .... save money on phone bills .... putting a timer on your phone.
5. .... save electricity, only put the water you need in the electric kettle.
6. .... you want to wake up at a certain time, say the time to yourself three times just before you go to sleep.
7. Don't thow old wine away; you .... always use it for cooking.
8. Save money .... shopping around to find where things are cheapest.
9. .... make tea taste better, warm the tea-leaves before you use them.

2 Write five sentences about ways of saving money.

....

....

....

....

....

....

....

3 Put the words in the right order.

1. boss tell I better my 'd . I'd better tell my boss.
2. we umbrellas had take better ? ....
3. not sweater had without better you out come a . ...
4. better police phone you think 'd I the . ...
5. not I anything better say 'd . ...
6. condition Andrew not better had his drive in . ...

Now make some sentences with *had better* for these situations.

1. A friend comes by and invites you to the cinema, but you're expecting an important phone call. What do you say? ....
2. It is very cold outside, and your husband/wife/friend is starting to walk out of the door in a shirt and trousers. What do you say? ....
3. A child wants to go to a party, but she is feeling ill and has a temperature. What does her father say? ....
4. You and a friend have to be at the airport in 15 minutes. It is five miles away and you have not left yet. What do you say? ....

4 Countable or uncountable? Put *a* or *some* before each word. Use your dictionary if you are not sure.

some money
a child
.... lake
.... heat
.... news
.... cough
.... job
.... fuel
.... dance
.... bag
.... luggage
.... tobacco
.... work
.... furniture

5 Revision. Study the examples, and then put *some* or *any* in each blank.

Examples:

There are some people here to see you.
There's some coffee in the pot.
Are there any pencils in that drawer?
Is there any milk in this cake?
Would you like some more meat?
Would you like some biscuits?

1. Are there .... birds in your garden?
2. There are .... lovely hills near where my aunt lives.
3. I'm afraid I haven't got .... free time this weekend at all.
4. Would you like .... newspapers to read while you're waiting?
5. 'Could you possibly lend me .... milk?' 'Sorry, I haven't got .... But why don't you ask Barry – I think he's got ....'

6 **Here is a food vocabulary network. Try to fill in the blanks.**

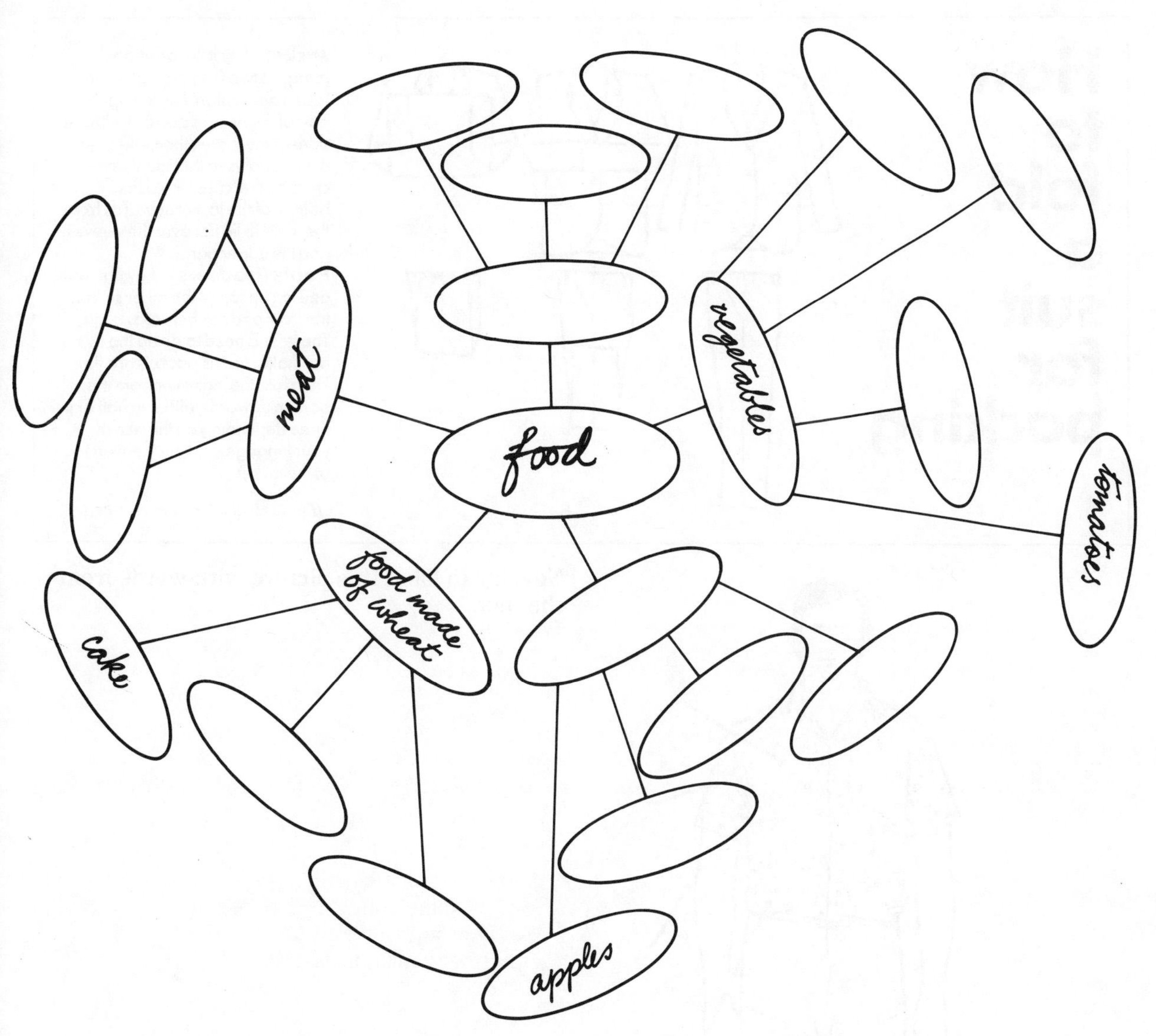

Now make a vocabulary network with DRINKS in the middle.

7 **Read the text *without* using your dictionary. Try to understand as much as you can by looking at the pictures that go with the text.**

How to fold a suit for packing

Jacket Lay it flat on its back, bring the two fronts together and fasten one button. Lay the upper part of the sleeves parallel with the sides of the jacket, then fold over at the elbows so that the sleeves cross on the 'chest'. Fold the bottom of the jacket upwards from the waist to lie flat over the sleeves and the upper part.

Pants (trousers) Lay flat, with one leg on top of the other so that the front and back creases align. There is no need to do up the fly, but make sure all pockets are flat. Then fold the legs over from the bottom upwards, either in half or in three depending on the size of your luggage, and lay them on top of the jacket.

(from *How to Hold a Crocodile* – adapted)

Now try to label this picture with words from the text.

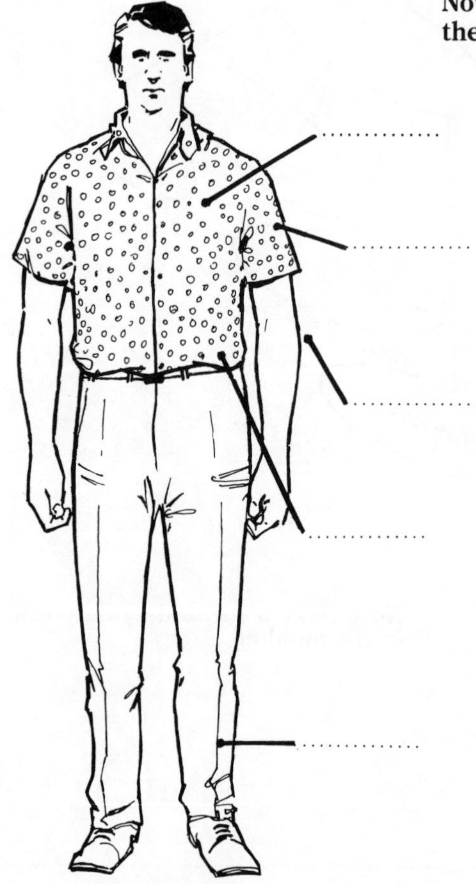

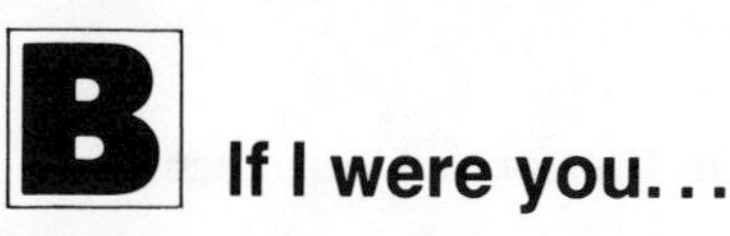

If I were you...

1 **Try to fill in the gaps in the letter without looking at the words in the box. Then look at the box for help with the words you could not guess.**

Dear Al,

.... a lot for your last letter. .... answered before; I've .... very busy getting ready to go to New York.

I .... about your trouble with Sally, especially because it's .... going on for so long. You .... try to make a decision soon, I think – it's bad for .... of you to go on like this. I think perhaps it would .... if you separated, but of course I might be .... – I don't know Sally very well.

You know, if .... I'd go away alone for a couple of .... If you were ...., you could think things out .... and decide what to do. .... take your holiday now and go off to Scotland or somewhere like that? I'm .... it would do you a lot of good.

Write again .... and let me know how things are going. And don't .... to kiss Julie for me. Ann sends her.......................... .

Yours,

Bill

be better been been both calmly
by yourself forget haven't to hear
I were you love ought to soon Sorry
sure Thanks weeks wrong
Why don't you

2 A friend of yours has a problem. For example: he or she doesn't like his or her job; or is having trouble with a parent/child/wife/husband/lover; or has money problems; or can't decide what to do after leaving school. Write a short letter giving your opinion. Use some of the words and expressions from the lesson.

3 How many things can you find wrong with this picture? Example:

The cakes are face downwards. ....

4 Revision. Put in the correct verb forms.

1. One of our windows was .... by the wind last night. (*break*)
2. This camera was .... in Czechoslovakia. (*make*)
3. 'What does Joan think about the changes?' 'She hasn't been .... yet.' (*tell*)
4. This was .... by a child. Look at the handwriting. (*write*)
5. Alice thinks her firm is in trouble. She hasn't been .... this month. (*pay*)
6. 'How's your new house?' 'It's still being .... We think it'll be finished in August.' (*build*)
7. 'That's a lovely necklace.' 'Yes, it was .... to me by my grandmother when I was eight.' (*give*)
8. English is .... here. (*speak*)
9. 'I heard you had an accident.' 'Yes, but nobody was ....' (*hurt*)

5 **Do you know how to form the past tenses (and past participles) of regular verbs? Try these verbs. If you have trouble remembering the rules, they are on page 143.**

join ...joined...
mend ...
cry ...
hate ...
predict ...
rub ...
fix ...
happen ...

need ...
empty ...
control ...
snow ...
guess ...
boil ...
explain ...
double ...

play ...
frighten ...
relax ...
apply ...
cough ...
improve ...
stay ...
prefer ...

Unit 21

Technology

A Electricity

1 **Can you complete the text with the words in the box?**

beating countryside dreaming electric electricity has to less running swimming television washing

To the man in the street, ... is the cause of a lightning flash, or the form of energy that powers his ... and ... machine. He knows that ... trains use electrical power and he is reminded of his dependence on it by the network of power lines criss-crossing the ..., or by a power cut, when he ... read by candlelight. But there are other ... well-known everyday processes that involve the use of electricity. A ... heart, a ... athlete, a ... baby and a ... fish all generate a form of electricity just as surely as a power station does.

2 Explain what these things are. Make sentences like this:

A(n) .... is a .... that ....

Example:

An orange is a fruit that grows in Africa.

orange	fruit	grows in Africa.
vacuum cleaner	person	makes distant things look nearer.
hospital	instrument	keeps food cool.
cat	machine	sick people go to.
telephone directory	animal	cleans floors.
fridge	book	catches mice.
doctor	machine	has phone numbers in.
house	appliance	takes people from place to place.
car	building	people live in.
telescope	building	cures people that are ill.

3 Do you know these irregular verbs?

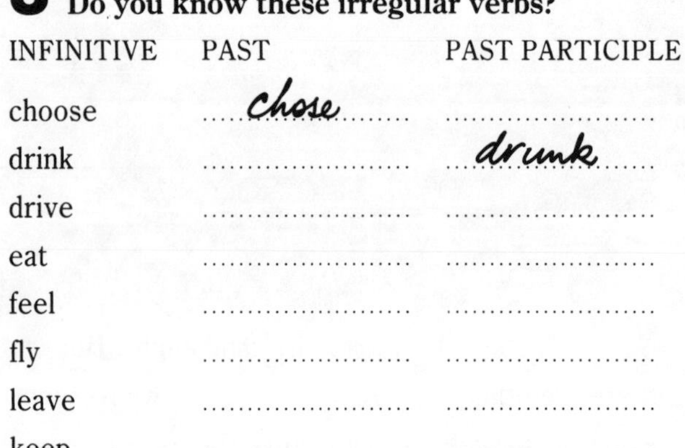

INFINITIVE	PAST	PAST PARTICIPLE
choose	*chose*	
drink		*drunk*
drive		
eat		
feel		
fly		
leave		
keep		

4 Put in the correct verb form.

1. If I ...*were*... you, I ...*would go*... home. (*be; go*)
2. If you married Peter, you .... a very unhappy life. (*have*)
3. I would tell you the answer if I .... (*know*)
4. If John .... sometimes, he would be much more attractive. (*smile*)
5. I .... German if I had time. (*learn*)
6. What would you do if I .... away? (*go*)
7. If you went away, I .... all my friends and have a party. (*invite*)
8. I .... Jane a postcard if I knew her address. (*send*)
9. Would you still love me if I .... a beard? (*grow*)
10. If I had enough money, I .... round the world. (*travel*)

5 If you could only have three things that worked by electricity, what would you choose? Why?

6 Read one or more of these texts with a dictionary.

Thanks to the electric light, Americans today, on the average, sleep 1½ hours less each day than Americans of six decades ago. A University of Florida report noted that most adults sleep 7½ hours a day and that about 15 percent sleep less than 6½ hours.

A chip of silicon a quarter-inch square has the capacity of the original 1949 ENIAC computer, which occupied a city block.

The world's smallest electric motor weighs one half-millionth of a pound and is smaller than the head of a pin. Built by a Californian, William McLellan, the motor measures a sixty-fourth of an inch on all sides. It has thirteen parts and generates one-millionth of a horsepower. It can be seen in operation only through a microscope. McLellan built the motor using a toothpick, a microscope, and a watchmaker's lathe.

In 1920, a Detroit policeman named William L. Potts worked out an electric light system that allowed him to control three street intersections from one tower. He picked the colours red, yellow, and green because railroads used them. These were the first street traffic lights.

An electron and a positron attract each other in two ways: the electromagnetic attraction of their opposite electric charges, and the gravitational attraction of their two masses. The electromagnetic attraction is 4,200,000,000,000,000,000,000,000,000,000,000,000,000,000 times as strong as the gravitational. (Of the four known forces – gravitation, weak interaction, electromagnetic interaction, strong interaction – the gravitational force is by far the weakest.)

The largest light bulb was a foot-long 75,000-watt bulb hand-blown at the Corning Glass Works to celebrate the seventy-fifth anniversary of Thomas Edison's invention of the incandescent lamp.

(from *The Book of Facts* by Isaac Asimov)

B It doesn't work

1 Read as much of this as you want. You can use a dictionary.

How to put things right

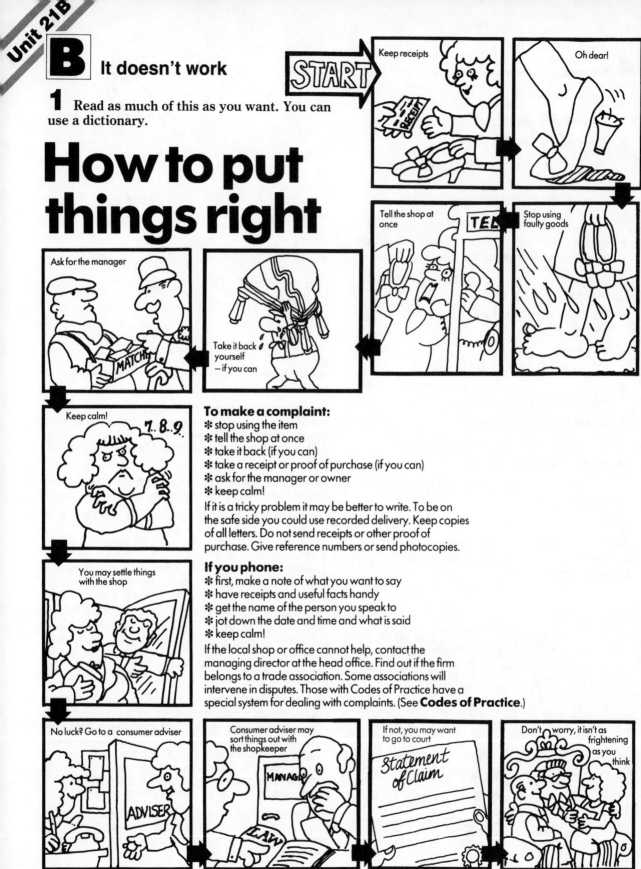

To make a complaint:

* stop using the item
* tell the shop at once
* take it back (if you can)
* take a receipt or proof of purchase (if you can)
* ask for the manager or owner
* keep calm!

If it is a tricky problem it may be better to write. To be on the safe side you could use recorded delivery. Keep copies of all letters. Do not send receipts or other proof of purchase. Give reference numbers or send photocopies.

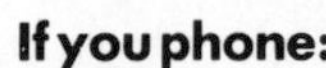

If you phone:

* first, make a note of what you want to say
* have receipts and useful facts handy
* get the name of the person you speak to
* jot down the date and time and what is said
* keep calm!

If the local shop or office cannot help, contact the managing director at the head office. Find out if the firm belongs to a trade association. Some associations will intervene in disputes. Those with Codes of Practice have a special system for dealing with complaints. (See **Codes of Practice**.)

(Her Majesty's Stationery Office)

2 **Separate the three mixed-up stories, and write one of them down. You can use a dictionary.**

Yesterday morning I dropped my watch on the bathroom floor. Once on holiday I drove up a muddy dirt road in a forest. It's a digital one, and when I picked it up it said '99:99', which was certainly not the right time. Last year my cousin was on a television programme. After about 20 minutes I got stuck in the mud. I took it to a jeweller's yesterday afternoon. That morning, our TV broke down completely – no picture, no sound. Of course we couldn't get anyone to repair it in such a short time. I just couldn't move. They said it would be ten days before I could get it back. We tried to rent one, but there were none available. After trying all sorts of things, I put an old blanket under the wheels and drove out over that. Luckily we found a neighbour who let us watch hers.

3 **Write a story about something that you bought that didn't work; or write a letter of complaint to a shop about something you bought that doesn't work. Use some of the new words and expressions that you have learnt.**

4 **Say when you started and stopped doing things. Examples:**

I started playing the piano when I was eight.

I stopped smoking five years ago.

5 **Make sentences with *by... ing*. Example:**

You can clean hair by washing it with shampoo.

You can clean hair	by washing it with shampoo.
You can fry eggs	by smiling at them.
You can save petrol	by warming it.
You can make shoe polish soft	by shopping around.
You can save money	by talking about yourself too much.
You can make tea taste better	by not driving fast.
You can make people happy	by heating them in butter.
You can lose friends	by warming the tea leaves before you pour the water on.

6 Try the crossword.

ACROSS

1. What do you do if the radio isn't loud enough?
5. Contraction of *I am.*
8. 'I'm sorry.' 'That's all ....'
9. I'll see you .... eight o'clock.
10. Unwell.
11. I'll see you .... Tuesday.
12. Not in.
13. 'Are you happy?' 'Yes, I ....'
15. It's .... to drive after drinking alcohol.
17. The opposite of *out of.*
19. Just like *11 across.*
21. Is this a long word?
23. You can use this machine to listen to yourself.

DOWN

1. Terrorism is his business.
2. Not wrong, not left.
3. The same as *17 across.*
4. The opposite of *pick up* is .... *down.*
6. 1,760 yards; 1.6 km.
7. You can see through it.
13. The number of years you have lived.
14. 'Excuse ...., can you help ....?'
15. Do, did, ...
16. The sun is one.
18. The high end of something.
20. 'Is John ready?' 'Yes, ... is.'
21. Is this different from *21 across*?
22. Would you like some food .... something to drink?

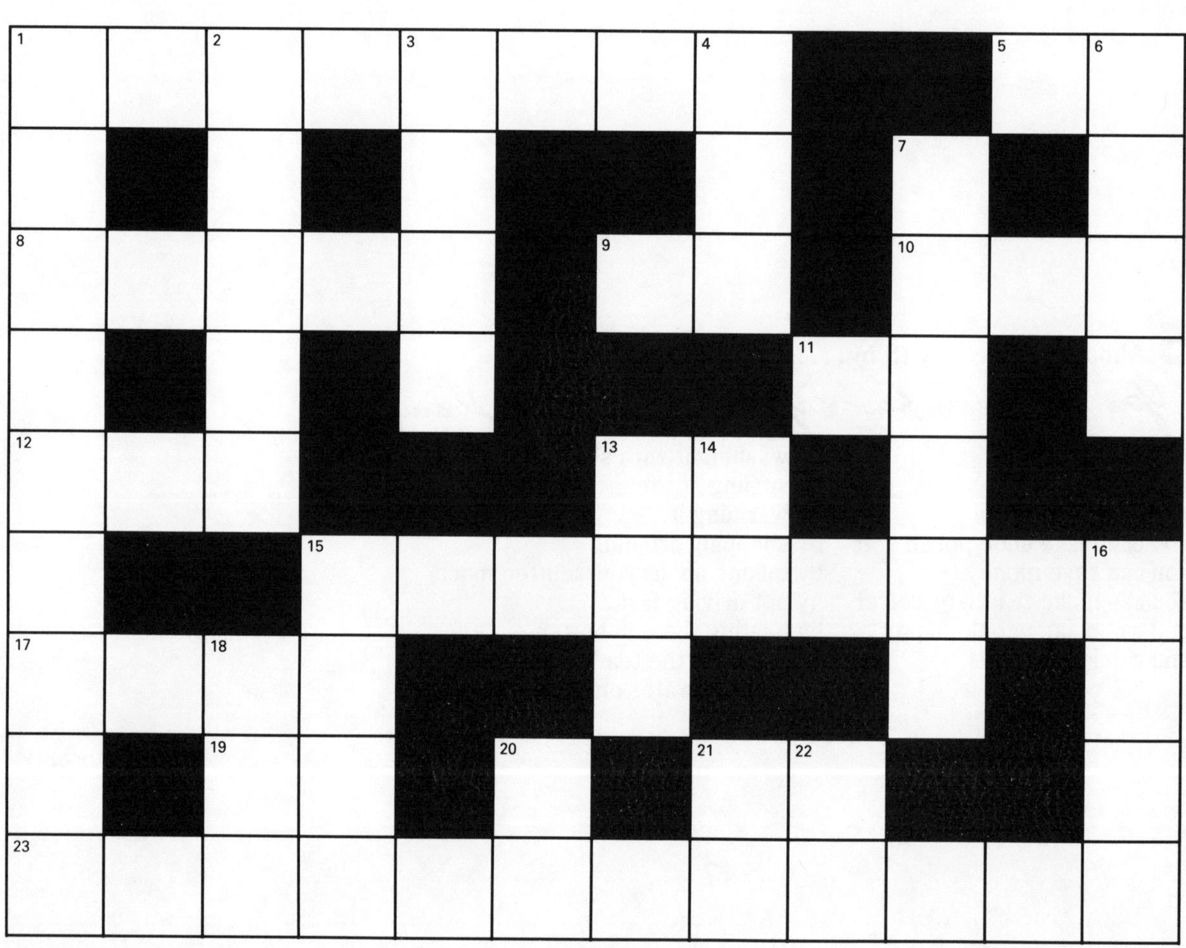

(Solution on page 144.)

THERE IS NO PRACTICE BOOK WORK FOR UNIT 22.

Feelings

A Not exactly calm

1 Make sentences with *let.*

1. I felt like crying. I didn't stop myself.
   I let myself cry.
2. Liz wants to go on the school skiing holiday, but her parents say it's too expensive.
   Liz's parents aren't going to let her go on the school skiing holiday.
3. Janet wanted to leave work early. Her boss said it was OK.
   ....
4. John asked his dad if he could go to the disco, and his dad agreed.
   ....
5. Julie's hair is growing long, and she's not going to cut it.
   ....
6. My brother makes his children go to bed at eight o'clock except on Friday and Saturday. Then they stay up late. ....
   ....
7. No one ever knows how Dunstan is feeling; he would rather keep his emotions to himself.
   ....
8. Ruth wanted to borrow Kate's car, and Kate said she could.
   ....
9. The fire went out because we didn't put any more wood on it.
   ....
10. Joan says to her children: 'You can wear anything you want as long as it's clean and comfortable.'
    ....
    ....

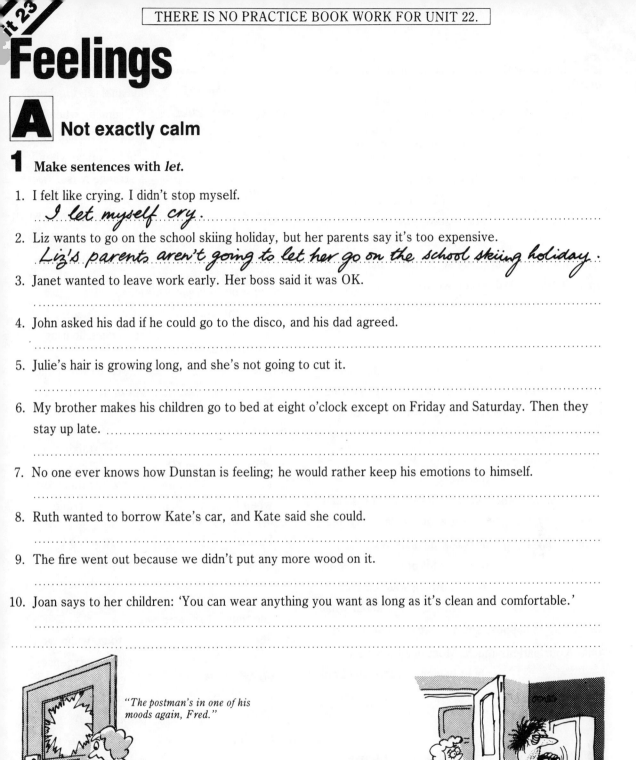

"The postman's in one of his moods again, Fred."

"Dad, you're shaving with my transistor radio."

2 Put one of the words from the box in each blank.

calm	changes	cried	cross	different
easy-going	ourselves	sad	shouted	
talked	upset	usual	went	worried

My mother and my father are very .... people. Mum is always very ....; not exactly ...., because she does take things very seriously sometimes, but she doesn't get excited. When we were small she almost never .... at us. When we did something wrong, she .... to us about it very firmly, but in a calm tone of voice. If we shouted and ...., she made us go and sit by .... in her sewing room until we calmed down. So when the news came, she reacted in her .... way, quietly seeing what she could do to prepare for the .... that were coming.

Dad, on the other hand, shouted, kicked a chair, and .... for a long walk to try and cool off. During the next few days he was .... with us a lot of the time, which .... us, as nothing was our fault. All of us kids were .... about what was going to happen, and a bit afraid, but we didn't talk to our parents much. Most of all we were .... about having to leave all of our school friends.

3 Put each verb in the correct past tense.

1. I was walking out of the door when the phone rang. (*walk*; *ring*)
2. When the phone rang, I put down my handbag and answered it. (*ring*; *put*; *answer*)
3. He was running very fast when he hurt his ankle. (*run*; *hurt*)
4. He stopped running when he hurt his ankle. (*stop*; *hurt*)
5. I .... in my office when I .... a strange noise. (*work*; *hear*)
6. We .... straight home when the party .... (*come*; *end*)
7. He .... out of his chair when the doctor .... into the room. (*jump*; *walk*)
8. After the music ...., I .... someone shouting downstairs. (*stop*; *hear*)
9. She .... cards when she .... get up to answer the door. (*play*; *have to*)
10. Geoff .... very interested when we .... talking about horses. (*get*; *start*)
11. I .... for a bus this morning when I .... a terrible accident. (*wait*; *see*)
12. I .... to bed when I .... home. (*go*; *get*)
13. She .... the phone as soon as it ...., but there was no one there. (*answer*; *ring*)
14. She .... to go when we .... to pay her expenses. (*agree*; *agree*)
15. It .... very hard when they .... (*rain*; *arrive*)
16. Her aunt .... while they .... in Libya. (*die*; *live*)

4 **Add more words to this vocabulary network.**

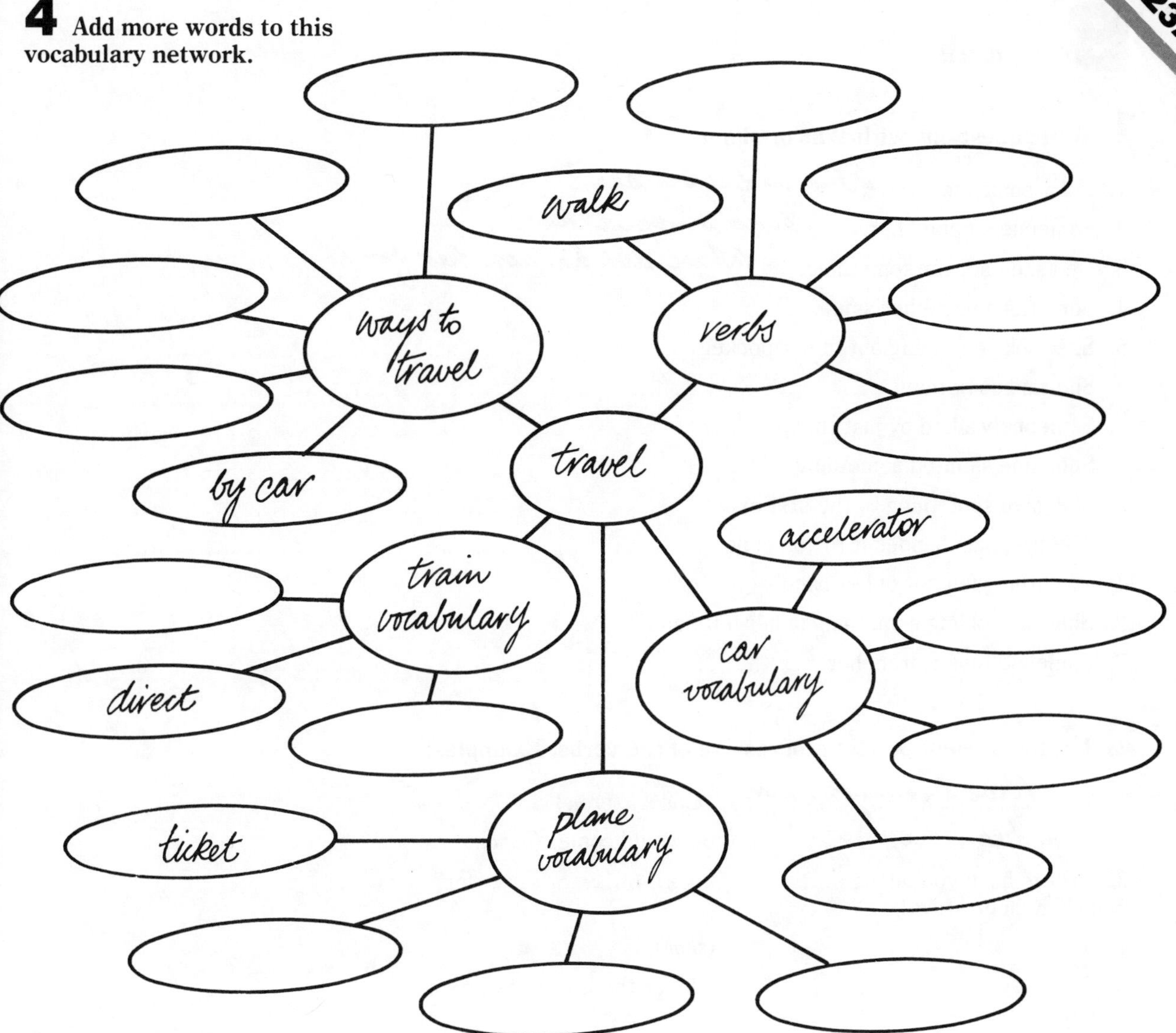

5 **Complete the first text, and write another text from the notes. Look at Exercise 5 in the Student's Book for help.**

I'm not a very .... person; I'm .... calm and easy-going. I don't often .... angry – I don't really see the point of it. And I almost never .... or .... When something .... me, I just try to see how I can change it. I don't let the people around me know how I .... unless there is a good reason for it. My emotions take a long time to build up, but they are strong and lasting.

NOTES

emotional but don't share moods
when upset, usually keep it inside instead of shouting/crying
would like to be more open about emotions
would feel more comfortable if I could express more
have never learnt to

Now write a few sentences about yourself or someone you know. Write about your/their emotions and how they are expressed.

Unit 23B

B In love

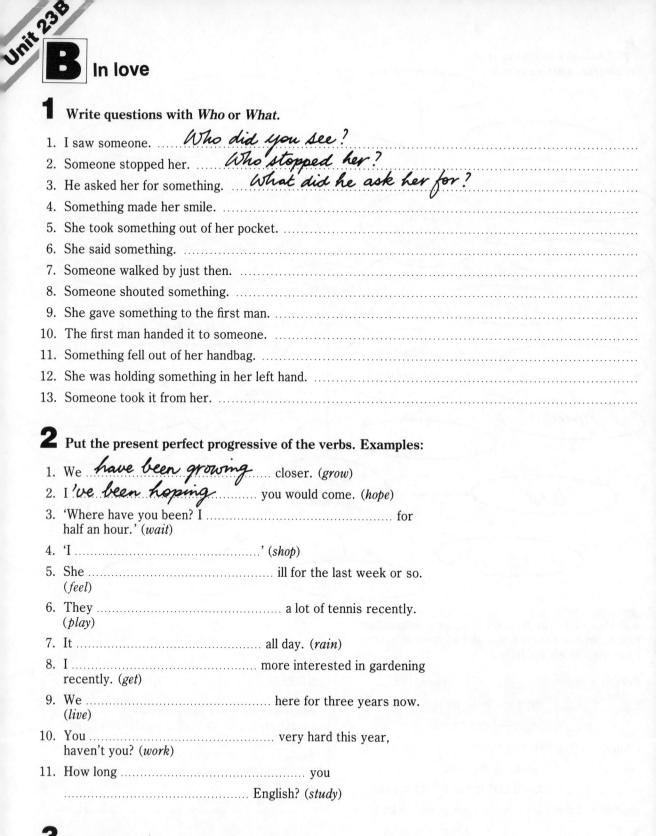

1 Write questions with *Who* or *What*.

1. I saw someone. *Who did you see?*
2. Someone stopped her. *Who stopped her?*
3. He asked her for something. *What did he ask her for?*
4. Something made her smile. ....
5. She took something out of her pocket. ....
6. She said something. ....
7. Someone walked by just then. ....
8. Someone shouted something. ....
9. She gave something to the first man. ....
10. The first man handed it to someone. ....
11. Something fell out of her handbag. ....
12. She was holding something in her left hand. ....
13. Someone took it from her. ....

2 Put the present perfect progressive of the verbs. Examples:

1. We *have been growing* closer. (*grow*)
2. I *'ve been hoping* you would come. (*hope*)
3. 'Where have you been? I .... for half an hour.' (*wait*)
4. 'I ....' (*shop*)
5. She .... ill for the last week or so. (*feel*)
6. They .... a lot of tennis recently. (*play*)
7. It .... all day. (*rain*)
8. I .... more interested in gardening recently. (*get*)
9. We .... here for three years now. (*live*)
10. You .... very hard this year, haven't you? (*work*)
11. How long .... you .... English? (*study*)

3 EITHER: Invent a problem letter to a magazine advice column OR: Write an answer to the letter from Philip in the Student's Book.

4 **Here are the words of a favourite song of the great American blues singer, Billie Holiday. Try reading them the first time without a dictionary.**

WHAT SHALL I SAY?

What shall I say
When our neighbours
Want us to come to tea?
They don't know you're not with me.
What shall I say?

What shall I say
When the phone rings
And someone asks for you?
They don't know I ask for you too.
What shall I say?

How can I hide the tears inside?
How can I face the crowd?
I can make lips of mine be still,
But my heart sighs too loud.

I could explain that
You're gone for only a week or two.
But after those weeks are through.
What shall I say?

(Words and music by Peter Tinturin)

"Gerald, I don't think our both being left-handed is enough."

5 **Grammar revision. Choose the correct pronoun in each case.**

1. Here's your towel, but where's *I/me/my/mine*?
2. I can't find the car keys – do you remember where you left *they/them/their/theirs*?
3. Where is *she/her/hers* from?
4. Could you ask Edward to bring *he/him/his* torch?
5. I'll ask the girls where *they/them/their/theirs* want to eat.
6. Didn't I meet *you/your/yours* in New York last December?
7. *We/Us/Our/Ours* house is not particularly old, but there are some very old houses in the village.
8. You and Denis didn't tell me that all this land was *you/your/yours*!
9. We waved at them from across the street, but I don't think they saw *we/us/our/ours*.
10. Where does the dog hide *it/its* bones?

6 **Spelling revision: *ie* or *ei*? Complete these words. Use your dictionary if you are not sure.**

bel ie f	interv . . w
d ie	n . . ghbour
ei ther	n . . ther
exper . . nce	n . . ce
f . . ld	p . . ce
fr . . ndship	sc . . nce
for . . gn	th . . f
h . . ght	w . . ght

Unit 24 Authority

A Government in Britain and the USA

1 Complete the text with words and expressions from the box.

HOW FANTASIA IS GOVERNED

Fantasia is a .... of three states: Moldenia, Stranvegan and East Mork. San Fantastico, the ...., is the centre of .... for the .... of Fantasia, but each state has its .... government. State governments make their own ...., and are .... for education, roads, health, the police and a number of other things.

Fantasia has 17 ....; there are very large .... between them. .... are held .... seven years. Each state sends 100 representatives to the federal ....

The Fantasian Parliament has little real .... The country is .... by a Council of 15 ministers (five from each ....), under the country's .... for life, Mrs Kirsten Rask.

capital differences elections every federation governed government laws own Parliament parties power President responsible state whole

2 Write about the system of government in your own country, or in another country that you know well.

3 Put in *can, could, will be able to* or *would be able to.*

1. My father .... speak eight languages, but he can't write any of them.
2. In another year I .... speak English pretty well, I think.
3. When I was younger I .... swim really fast.
4. If we were at home now we .... ask Martin what he thinks.
5. I .... walk when I was one year old, but I ....n't talk until I was three.
6. If you didn't spend so much money on cigarettes you .... buy a car.
7. I can't tell you anything now, but I .... give you some information tomorrow.
8. .... you understand what she's saying?

"But if you leave politics, my pet, what would you do? You're too stupid to do anything else."

4 Can you finish these sentences?

If I was on the moon, ...

If the sun was as small as an orange, ...

If cats were as big as people, ...

If I spoke perfect English, ...

If I had more money, ...

If you invited me to have a drink with you, ...

If I were younger, ...

If animals could speak, ...

5 Countable or uncountable nouns? Put these words in the right list.

(Countable nouns can be used with *a/an*, and have plurals. Uncountable nouns cannot be used with *a/an*, and have no plurals.)

dust electricity fridge heat heater
heel knee leather metal onion
plastic plug rabbit rice
thunderstorm vinegar water

COUNTABLE	UNCOUNTABLE
cooker	wine
hair dryer	music
house	meat
idea	intelligence
shirt	milk
....	....
....	....
....	....
....	....
....	....
....	....
....	....
....	....
....	....

6 Read this with a dictionary.

MURPHY'S LAW, AND OTHER LAWS OF NATURE

If something can go wrong, then it will go wrong. ('Murphy's Law')

Nothing is as easy as it looks.

If you start to do something, you always find that there is something else which has to be done first.

If you explain so clearly that nobody can misunderstand, somebody will.

Most things get worse all the time.

Anything that begins well ends badly.

Anything that begins badly ends worse.

If it looks easy, it's difficult. If it looks difficult, it's impossible.

As soon as you talk about something:
if it's good, it goes away.
if it's bad, it happens.

However many socks you have, three of them are always the same colour.

Everywhere is uphill on a bicycle.

Cars prefer to break down on Sundays.

Officials make work for each other.

Those who can, do. Those who can't, teach.

Nothing is impossible for the man who doesn't have to do it himself.

Everything good in life is either illegal, immoral or fattening.

You can always find what you're not looking for.

When something breaks down, there are always two things wrong. You will only find one of them.

The lift is always on another floor.

Machines that have broken down will work perfectly when the repairman arrives.

Having baths makes telephones ring.

"I can say we live in a fascist state if I want to. It's a free country."

Unit 24B

B All right, I suppose so

1 Complete the sentences with question-tags.

1. You're not going to invite him, are you?
2. You won't play your father's jazz records, ...
3. He doesn't like pop music, ...
4. You haven't got £5 on you, ...
5. You won't be late home tonight, ...
6. She can't swim, ...
7. Your mother isn't religious, ...
8. John wasn't at the party, ...
9. Mary doesn't know I'm here, ...

2 Put in *have to, has to, had to* or *will have to.*

1. Most people .... work for a boss.
2. I haven't got any money now. I .... pay you tomorrow.
3. When I was 18, I .... do military service.
4. My father .... go to Scotland three or four times a year.
5. We .... talk about money soon.
6. He's lucky. He doesn't .... work.
7. I .... stay up very late last night.
8. In Britain people .... drive on the left.
9. In some countries everybody .... carry an identity card.

3 Make sentences with the present perfect progressive tense.

1. How long | you | wait? How long have you been waiting?
2. I | try | to write to him all day. I've been trying to write to him all day.
3. We | live in this house for about 12 years. ....
4. Janet | practise the violin all afternoon. ....
5. I | wait for a letter from my father for weeks. ....
6. How long | you | learn English? ....
7. People | fight each other for millions of years. ....
8. They | talk for a long time. ....
9. It | rain since I got up this morning. ....

4 **Some of these words are stressed on the first syllable (like *capital*), and some are stressed on the second syllable (like *authority*). Divide them into two groups, according to the stress, and then practise pronouncing them. Use a dictionary to help you if necessary.**

admire afraid amused authority capital carpet department delivery dislike elect emotion exactly express government invite local majority minister programme promise relationship relaxed responsible secret suppose urgent

5 **What do these road signs tell you to do or not to do? Examples:**

Sign A tells you to turn left.
Sign B tells you not to park.

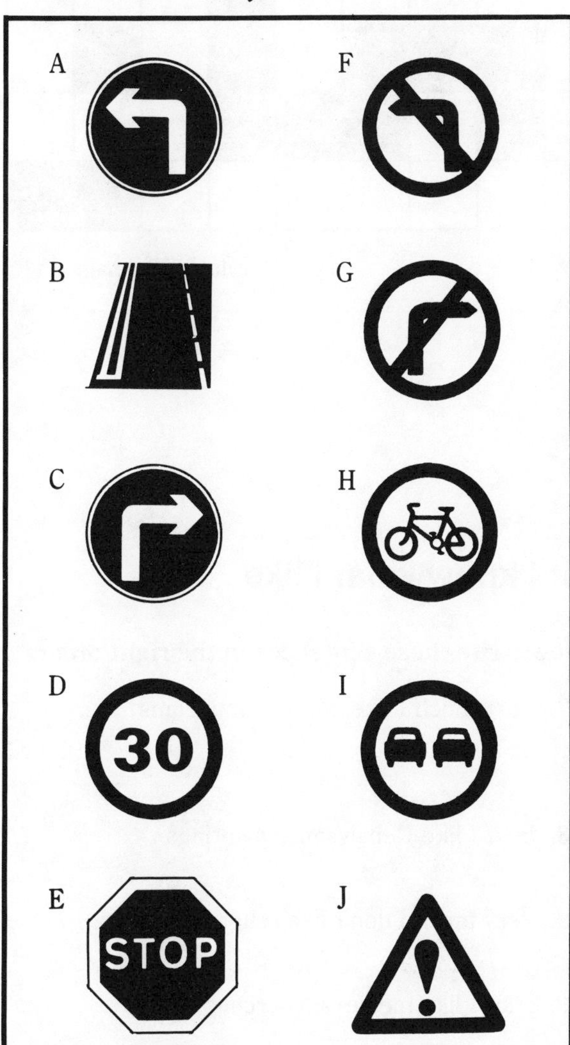

6 **Read this with a dictionary.**

Misleading advice for foreigners

[The *New Statesman* magazine set a competition in which readers were asked to give misleading advice to tourists visiting England for the first time. These are some of the entries.]

Women are not allowed upstairs on buses; if you see a woman there, ask her politely to descend.

Visitors in London hotels are expected by the management to hang the bedlinen out of the windows to air.

Try the famous echo in the British Museum Reading Room.

On first entering an underground train, it is customary to shake hands with every passenger.

If you take a taxi, the driver will be only too willing to give your shoes a polish while waiting at the traffic-lights.

Never attempt to tip a taxi-driver.

Public conveniences are few; unfrequented streets where relief is permitted are marked 'P'.

Parking is permitted in the grounds of Buckingham Palace on payment of a small fee to the sentry.

Never pay the price demanded for a newspaper; good-natured haggling is customary.

public conveniences: public lavatories
unfrequented: deserted
sentry: soldier on guard
haggling: arguing about the price

7 **Write some misleading advice for foreign tourists visiting your country. Use some of the words and expressions from the text in Exercise 6.**

8 Try the crossword.

ACROSS

1. Power over people.
6. Would you like a cup of ....?
7. The person that you work for.
9. Governing group.
11. United Nations.
12. You and I.
14. Six months before October.
15. Stop if the traffic lights are this colour.
17. Six months after November.
18. 'Can I have a party?' 'Yes, I .... so.'

DOWN

1. After that.
2. Person you learn from.
3. The opposite of *off*.
4. Do you .... your shirts yourself?
5. The day after the day before yesterday.
7. You put rubbish in this.
8. Put buttons on a shirt.
10. Make a house.
13. The .... Minister is the head of the government.
16. What time did you get .... this morning?

1		2		3		4		5
6					7		8	
		9		10				
				11			12	
						13		
14						15		
		16				17		
18								

(Solution on page 144.)

Unit 25

Look and listen

I don't know much about art, but I know what I like

1 Some of these sentences have got words in the wrong order. Correct the sentences that are wrong, and put 'OK' after the correct sentences.

1. I like very much modern art.
2. Of all the impressionists, I like Manet best.
3. I don't like Giacometti's statues much.
4. I don't like very much Van Gogh.
5. I like best Picasso's early paintings.
6. I like some abstract paintings a lot.

Now write these sentences in the right order.

7. very much I like going to museums . ...
....
8. best I like Renaissance paintings . ...
....
9. very much I don't like religious paintings . .....
....
10. a lot I like medieval churches . ...
....

2 Put in *very* or *too*.

1. You are looking .... beautiful this evening.
2. Oh no! We're .... late! The museum's closed!
3. You are .... young to remember how beautiful this city was before the war.
4. Leonardo da Vinci was not only a .... great painter; he was also a scientist and an engineer.
5. I'm .... pleased that we were able to see those Nigerian statues.
6. You should be careful about oil paintings around central heating; if the air gets .... dry, they can crack.
7. Is Geoffrey .... upset about not getting into art school?

3 See if you can make up some questions ending in *by* for these answers.

1. Charlotte Brontë.
   Who was Jane Eyre written by?
2. Gustave Eiffel.
   ....
   ....
3. Michelangelo.
   ....
   ....
4. Shakespeare.
   ....
   ....
5. Tolstoy.
   ....
   ....
6. Alfred Hitchcock.
   ....
   ....

4 Strange but true. Read this with a dictionary.

The largest picture ever painted was *Panorama of the Mississippi*, by John Banvard (1815–1891). It was about 1,500m long and 3.65m wide. It was destroyed in a fire.

Velazquez' painting *Portrait of Juan de Pareja* was sold for £2,310,000 in 1970. In 1801 the same painting had been sold for £40.95.

Picasso produced about 13,500 paintings and drawings, as well as large numbers of book illustrations, prints, sculptures and ceramics.

If you visit all the parts of the Hermitage Museum in Leningrad you have to walk 24 kilometres.

Paintings have been found in caves in France that are 27,000 years old.

The Museum of Modern Art in New York hung *Le Bateau* by Matisse upside down for 47 days before they discovered their mistake.

(Above information from *The Guinness Book of Records*)

Professor Marguerita Guarducci of Rome has shown that some of the so-called 'ancient' objects in the Louvre, the British Museum, the Boston Museum of Fine Arts and Rome's Museum of Prehistory were actually made by two nineteenth-century criminals.

(Information from an article by Tana de Zulueta in *The Sunday Times*)

In 1981 a British gallery showed a work called *Room Temperature*: two dead flies and a bucket of water in which four apples and six empty balloons were floating. A gallery official was enthusiastic about the work's 'completeness, its oneness, its apparent obviousness'.

(Information from an article in *The International Herald Tribune*)

5 Circle the one that is different.

1. painting statue (switch) drawing
2. jazz rock folk music violin
3. swim eat run jump
4. hungry tired thirsty exciting
5. laugh frown worried smile
6. glove shoe chair sock
7. England Scotland Ireland Wales
8. hair dryer vacuum cleaner hairbrush food mixer
9. bottom inside out face downwards sideways

(Solution on page 144.)

6 Grammar revision. Put in the right form of the verb.

1. 'What are you doing?' 'I ....' (*shave*)
2. We often .... walking on Sundays. (*go*)
3. 'Can I help you?' 'Yes. I .... my keys.' (*lose*)
4. We .... August in Scotland most years, but this year we went to Jersey. (*spend*)
5. My wife doesn't usually .... home at lunchtime. (*come*)
6. I didn't know you .... German. (*speak*)
7. Telephone me when you .... to London. (*come*)
8. Everybody .... Janet. (*like*)

B Quite a choice

1 Put in *which* or *what.*

1. .... colour are her eyes?
2. .... colour do you prefer – green or blue?
3. .... time is your train?
4. .... train are you getting – the 4.15 or the 5.33?
5. You can come at half past three, four o'clock or half past four. .... time would suit you?
6. .... sort of books do you read?
7. '............ is the hot tap?' 'The one on the right.'
8. '............ door goes to the kitchen?' 'That one.'
9. .... languages do you speak?

2 Answer these questions using *one* or *ones.*

1. Several teachers from your school are standing together. Someone asks you, 'Which one is your English teacher?' What do you answer?
2. You are standing at the door of your classroom. Someone asks you, 'Which chair/desk do you usually sit in?' What do you answer?
3. You are packing a suitcase to go on a journey. A lot of your clothes are laid out on your bed. Someone asks you, 'Which is your favourite shirt/blouse/dress/sweater?' What do you answer?
4. If you had a lot of money to buy a car, what sort of car would you buy?
5. What kind of chairs do you prefer to sit in?

3 Put the sentences of this dialogue in the right order.

A: Why don't we go to the Goldie Hawn one? I loved her in *Private Benjamin.*
A: I don't really know what's on. Have we got a newspaper?
A: OK. Just let me comb my hair and I'll be ready to go.
A: Shall we go and see a film tonight?
A: Oh, not too serious – I've had a hard day.
B: Yeah, somewhere around here. Let me see. Oh, here we are. Do you feel like something serious or not?
B: Yeah, let's. What shall we see?
B: Well, what about the new *Superman* film at the Odeon? Or there's that new one with Goldie Hawn at the Crystal.
B: That sounds fine to me. It's not until 8.15. How about a quick Chinese meal beforehand?

....
....
....
....
....
....
....
....
....
....

4 Revision. Put the correct preposition in each blank.

about after at by from in near off on to with

1. I got a birthday card in the post this morning, but I don't know who it was ....
2. Why don't we go out for a drink .... the play?
3. What do you usually do .... the evening?
4. I've been reading this book for an hour, and I'm still not sure what it's ....
5. We'll be arriving .... Saturday the 9th .... around ten in the morning.
6. Can you be here .... 7.15? You can come earlier, of course, if that's easier.
7. Is your house .... the station, or do you have a long walk in the morning?
8. Are you coming .... us tomorrow, or do you prefer to stay here?
9. I wonder if you could take your books .... the table so I can put this down?
10. Have you ever been .... Egypt?

5 Revision. Put in the right verb forms.

1. Our house .... in 1493. (*build*)
2. We think this .... by Van Gogh. (*paint*)
3. The letter looks as if it .... by a child. (*write*)
4. Every time I go through customs I .... (*search*).
5. The best whisky .... in Scotland. (*produce*)
6. Too many books .... – nobody has time to read them all. (*publish*)
7. Her telephone .... because she didn't pay the bill. (*cut off*)
8. Do you know when that window ....? (*break*)
9. On Sundays our TV .... at breakfast time and it stays on all day. (*switch on*)

6 What is your favourite sort of art or music? How did you first become interested in it? If you had a lot of money to spend on this interest, how would you spend the money? Write eight sentences or more.

....

....

....

....

....

....

....

....

....

....

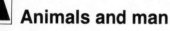

Different kinds

A Animals and man

1 Complete the text with words and expressions from the box.

.... of the languages of Europe – and some Middle-Eastern and Indian .... – are .... to each other. They .... to a large family which linguists call the 'Indo-European' .... of languages. .... they may look and sound completely .... from each other, linguists can show that their grammar and vocabulary are similar in many .... The Indo-European languages can be .... into eight .... groups: Germanic (................................ English); Romance (the languages which are descended from Latin, for example Spanish); Celtic (for example Scottish Gaelic); Balto-Slavonic (for example Russian); Indo-Iranian (for example Hindi, Farsi); Greek, Albanian and Armenian. Not .... European languages .... to the Indo-European family. Finnish and Hungarian, ..., are members of a quite .... language family, and Basque (spoken in northern Spain and south-western France) seems to be .... different from all the other languages in the ....

all although belong belong completely different different divided family for example including languages main most related ways world

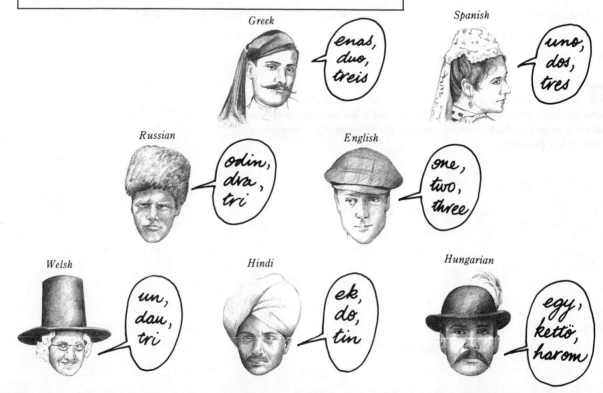

2 **Read the text about the Romance languages. Then write a text about the Germanic and Celtic languages. Use the notes to help you.**

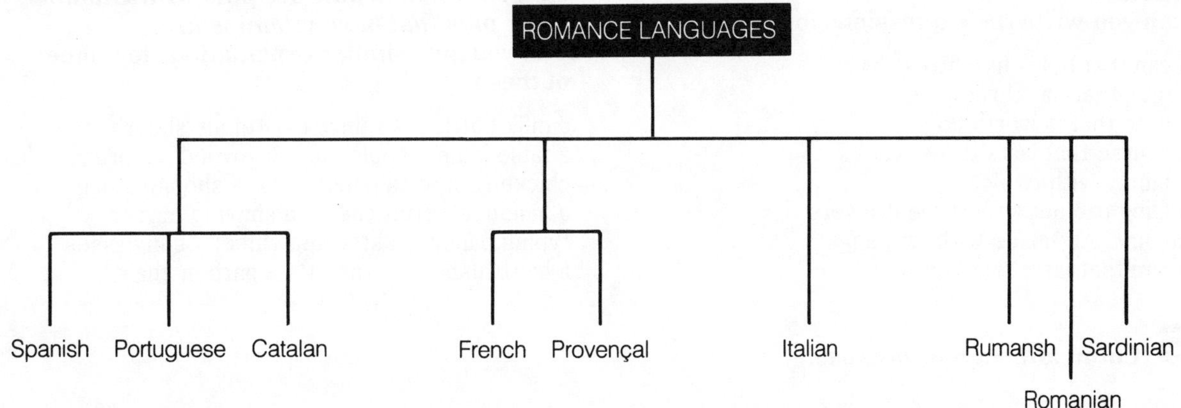

The Romance languages are all descended from Latin. They are divided into several groups by linguists. One group includes Spanish, Portuguese and Catalan. Another group contains French and Provençal. A third group contains the various dialects of Italian. Three other Romance languages which do not belong in these groups are Romanian, Rumansh (spoken in a part of Switzerland), and the language of Sardinia.

GERMANIC LANGUAGES

northern group: Icelandic, Danish, Norwegian, Swedish

western group: English, German, Dutch & Flemish

CELTIC LANGUAGES

Scottish Gaelic, Irish Gaelic, Manx

Welsh, Breton, Cornish

NOTES

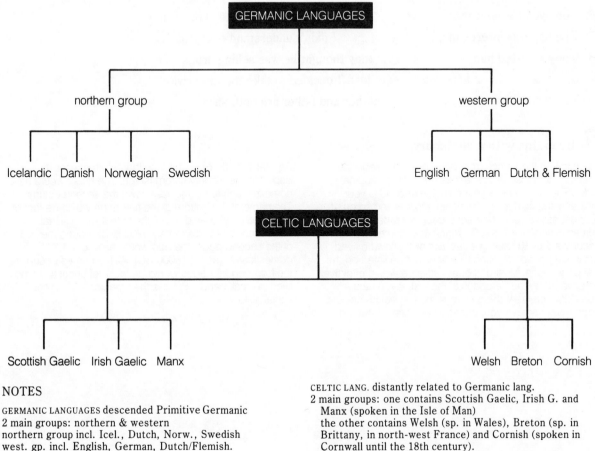

GERMANIC LANGUAGES descended Primitive Germanic
2 main groups: northern & western
northern group incl. Icel., Dutch, Norw., Swedish
west. gp. incl. English, German, Dutch/Flemish.

CELTIC LANG. distantly related to Germanic lang.
2 main groups: one contains Scottish Gaelic, Irish G. and Manx (spoken in the Isle of Man)
the other contains Welsh (sp. in Wales), Breton (sp. in Brittany, in north-west France) and Cornish (spoken in Cornwall until the 18th century).
So English closely related to German, but only distantly related to other languages of Britain.

3 A stamp that costs 13p is *a 13p stamp*. A holiday that lasts three days is *a three-day holiday*. Can you write the expressions for:

a can that holds five litres
a plug that has three pins
a note that is worth £5
a course that lasts three weeks
a family with two cars
a filing cabinet with three drawers
an omelette made with two eggs
a film that lasts two hours

4 A washing machine is *a machine for washing clothes*, or *a machine that washes clothes*. Vitamin pills are *pills with vitamins in*, or *pills that have vitamins in*. Can you give similar explanations for some of these?

a milk bottle   a raincoat   tennis shoes
a table lamp   apple pie   firewood   a breadknife
chicken soup   a paper hat   a shopping bag
a handbag   fruit cake   a shaving mirror
typing paper   a steering wheel   sunglasses
a hairbrush   a bathmat   a garden chair

5 Put in *although* or *because*.

1. .... she was ill for a long time, she lost her job.
2. .... he worked very well, he lost his job.
3. I like you .... you're funny.
4. She loved him .... he had a very difficult personality.
5. .... it was only three o'clock, we decided to stop work.
6. I enjoyed the holiday, ... the weather was a bit too hot for me.
7. The film was interesting, ... I didn't understand everything.
8. They arrested him .... they thought he was selling drugs.
9. .... I didn't want to get lost, I decided to take the motorway.
10. I'm very tall, ... my mother and father are both short.

6 Read this with a dictionary.

Imagine that the names on a page of a city telephone directory are those of your ancestors in chronological order. The first name is your own, the second is your mother's, the third is your mother's mother and so on. If your ancestors could be traced back over the whole of human history (say 750,000 years) their names would occupy about 100 such pages. But all those who lived within the period of written history would be listed on the first page alone. Most of modern science would effectively be covered by the life-spans of the first seven names – about 200 years. At the bottom of the first column would appear the name of your ancestor who lived in the Iron Age (about 720 BC – the time that Shalmaneser V deported the Hebrews from Israel). The horse would have come into service some way down the second column. The name at the bottom of the first page would be that of an ancestor who lived about the time the first sizeable city was founded (approximately 5200 BC). Around the bottom of the second page, the dog would have been domesticated (about 15000 BC). All the names occupying the following 98 pages would be those of ancestors who lived in small bands. Such is the time scale of human social history.

(from *Joy of Knowledge* by Dr Alex Comfort – adapted)

B It's a good one

1 This text has three paragraphs. In each paragraph, some words have been taken out. Can you put the words back? (There is one word too many in each box.)

There are about 4,500 kinds of .... These can be divided into 19 groups – .... call them orders – for instance the carnivores, or .... Typical .... are dogs, tigers or polar bears.

birds carnivores mammals meat-eaters scientists

.... is a mammal, belonging to the order called primates. There are several different kinds of ...., including monkeys (which have ....), and apes (which do not). Most primates live in .... They have hands and large ...., and can communicate very well.

brains mammals man primates tails trees

We are closely related to ...., and are very like them in most ways. Nobody knows exactly when the first people appeared, but 4–5 .... years ago there were .... primates in Africa. One and a .... million years ago there were .... primates which were very like us. The first .... which are certainly of modern man date from about half a million years ....

ago apes half hundred man-like meat-eating million skeletons

2 Can you divide these into groups?

1. Essential, useful or not very useful (to you).

ashtray button cushion feather fork hat knife paper pencil picture plate safety-pin soap stone toothpaste towel typewriter

2. Good, bad or neither.

asleep egg-shaped frightened hard hollow liquid long loud loving pretty relaxed sexy six-legged soft ugly useful wooden

3 Say whether the words in italics are nouns, verbs or adjectives.

1. Is the shop *open*?
2. Can you *open* this tin for me?
3. I'd like to *book* a table for dinner, please.
4. Is this your *book*?
5. Have you got any *paper* handkerchiefs?
6. Have you got today's *paper*?
7. We're going to *paper* the sitting room next weekend.
8. Do you *iron* your own shirts?
9. I've never travelled behind the *Iron* Curtain.
10. *Iron* melts at 1,539 degrees centigrade.

4 *The* or no article?

1. ...—... tigers are related to cats.
2. Where did you buy ...the... wine? It's very good.
3. .... wine is made from .... grapes.
4. The house is very quiet now that .... children have left home.
5. I don't really understand how .... electricity works.
6. We couldn't watch TV last night because .... electricity was cut off.
7. .... potatoes are terribly expensive these days.
8. Where did you put .... potatoes? I can't find them.
9. I'm quite good at .... languages, but I'm no good at all at .... mathematics.
10. Who are .... people you've invited to dinner?

5 Put in *because, although* or *that's why.*

1. .... I like most fish, I can't stand trout.
2. You're getting fat .... you don't take enough exercise.
3. My husband and I work in different places. .... we need two cars.
4. .... the weather's been so bad, we haven't been out of the house much.
5. Salaries are much better in America. .... John went to Washington.
6. I know why you like me. It's .... I make you laugh.
7. I don't really know Scotland, ... I did spend a week in Edinburgh once.
8. 'Why don't you go and see a film?' '........................... I haven't got any money.'
9. .... he doesn't work very fast, he gets a lot done.

6 Put in *there is/are, there was/were, there has/have been, there will be* or *there would be.*

1. .... about 3,000 different languages in the world.
2. The newspaper says .... rain tomorrow.
3. I think .... somebody at the door.
4. .... enormous changes in our village since I was a child.
5. Two hundred years ago .... no cars, no trains and no planes.
6. .... enough houses for everybody if the government was doing its job.
7. Have you heard the news? .... a revolution in Fantasia.
8. Yesterday evening .... a bad road accident just outside our house.

7 Can you divide these sentences into two groups according to their rhythm?

Ann took John shopping.
Please don't tell Mother.
It's nice to look at.
Ted's just stopped smoking.
She's gone to Moscow.
The meal was perfect.
Joan likes loud music.
We knew you had it.
I don't believe you.
Cats don't like swimming.

□□□□▫
Ann took John shopping.
....
....
....
....

▫□▫□▫
It's nice to look at.
....
....
....
....

Unit 27

Changes

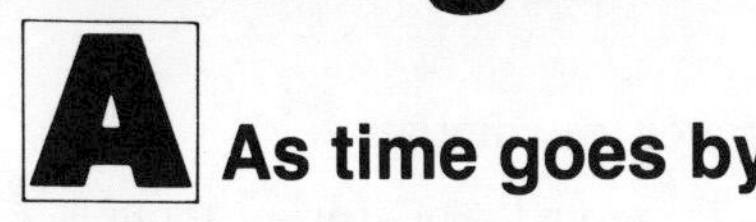

A As time goes by

1 Think of someone you know well. How has he or she changed over the past ten years? Write at least four sentences.

2 This car hasn't been looked after. What's the matter with it? Write five sentences.

3 Read this text without a dictionary and see how much you can understand. Then note down the words you don't know. Which ones can you guess the meanings of? Look up the words you can't guess, and read the text again.

News has come from America that we shall soon have no more children. The idea that children are different sorts of people from adults, says Mr Neil Postman, has not always been around. In medieval times most children did not go to school, but joined in adult life and entertainment.

Then printed books were invented, and became common. (Before that, the only books were copied by hand, and there were very few of them.) With printing, all families could have books: this meant that adults could get knowledge that children could not, since the children had to learn to read first. So some knowledge became unsuitable for children. They were no longer just small grown-ups, but had to learn to become grown-ups.

All this, says Mr Postman, is now changing. Printing created childhood, but television is destroying it once again. No one needs to *learn* to watch television. All knowledge is there for everyone to have. We are going to return to a medieval life-style, and children are once more going to be a part of the adult world.

4 Grammar revision. Put one word or expression from the box into each blank. You will not use all the words and expressions, and you may use some of them more than once.

am	as	by	for	has	have
have got	in	since	than	that	to

1. My sister's much taller .... I am.
2. Joan's been in Japan .... three months now.
3. I .... very cold – can we turn the heating on?
4. Have you got some liquid .... polishing furniture?
5. You can probably get a message to Ian .... phoning his sister.
6. I don't remember that it was .... cold .... this last year.
7. We .... some beer in the fridge if you want it.
8. I haven't seen my brother .... April.
9. I usually get up early to work and then stop and .... breakfast at about ten o'clock.

5 Write the correct form of *say* or *tell* in each blank.

1. When I was younger, my mother .... me a lot of stories about her childhood.
2. She often .... that her family was very poor, but that she didn't realise it.
3. She .... her mother was a very good cook and seamstress, and very well organised.
4. My grandmother had nine children, but mother .... she always kept the house clean and tidy.
5. Mother knew that if grandmother .... her to go and find a dish towel on the right-hand side of the third drawer in the chest of drawers in the hall, that's exactly where she would find it.
6. Grandmother made all the children's clothes, and she thought she was lucky to have a sewing maching (not an electric one!). She .... that *her* mother had made all *her* clothes by hand.
7. Of course the children helped with the housework. Mother liked to .... me that her brothers had to iron clothes and wash dishes just like the girls.

"Old age is his trouble – he used to leap through them!"

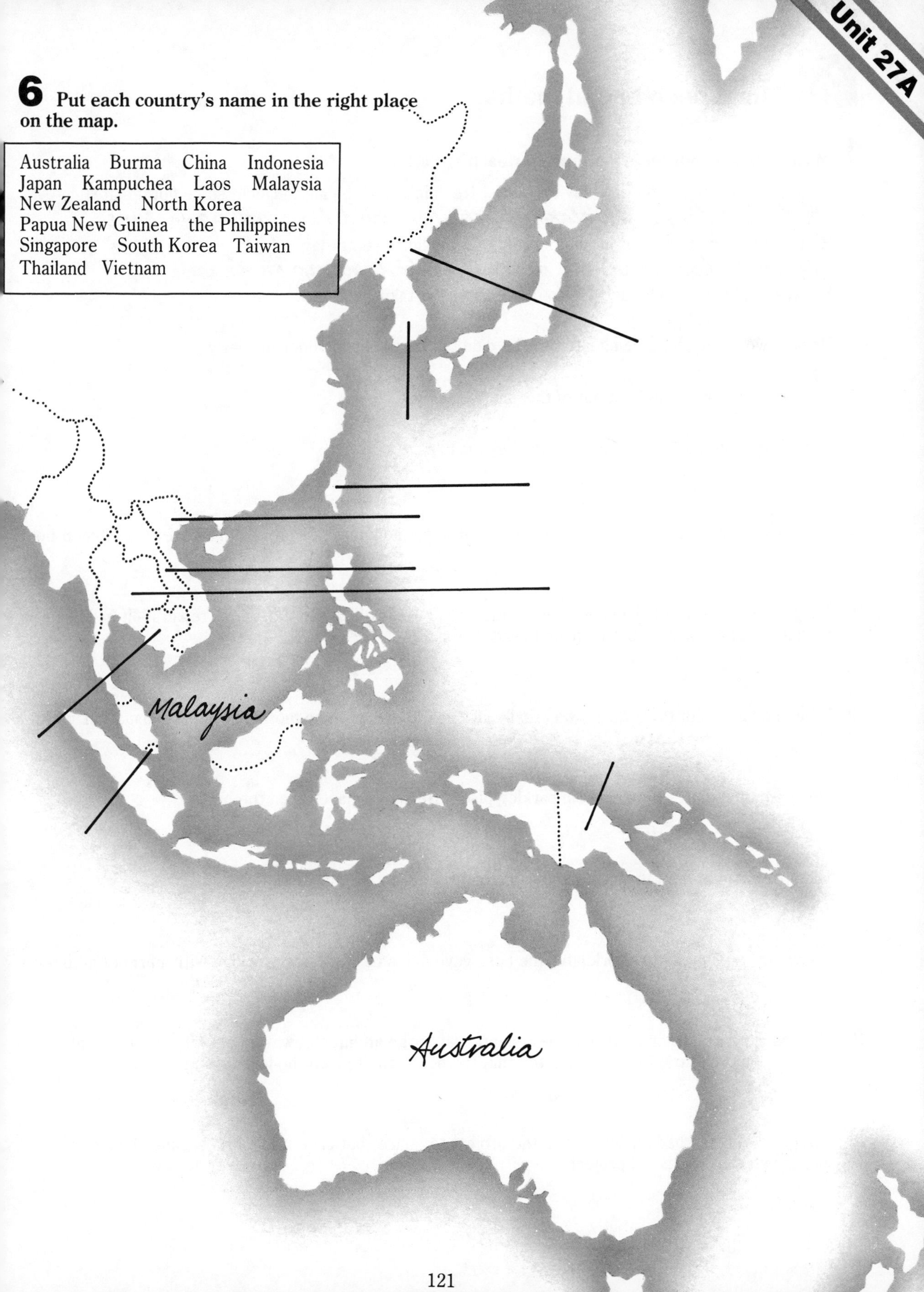
6 Put each country's name in the right place on the map.
Australia Burma China Indonesia
Japan Kampuchea Laos Malaysia
New Zealand North Korea
Papua New Guinea the Philippines
Singapore South Korea Taiwan
Thailand Vietnam
Malaysia
Australia

B If he'd been bad at maths...

1 Write a past conditional sentence for each situation.

1. Yesterday began as a terrible day for Chris. He didn't hear the alarm clock, so he got up late.
If he had heard the alarm clock, he would have got up on time.
2. He usually reads the paper in the morning, but he didn't yesterday.
He would have read the paper if he had got up on time.
3. He was really late, so he decided to drive instead of taking the bus.
....
4. He was worrying about being late, and he didn't close the house door properly.
....
5. He saw it was open, and got out of the car to close it.
....
6. In his hurry, he locked the car with the keys inside.
....
....
7. He ran back into the house to get the other car key, and knocked a jar of jam all over the kitchen floor.
....
....
8. He got stuck in a traffic jam because the main road to his office was closed for repairs – it had been in the paper that morning, but he hadn't read the paper.
....
....
9. When he finally got to work, he was really late, and there were no more places in his usual car park.
....
....
10. He spent 20 minutes looking for a parking place. He should have taken the bus!
....
....
11. His boss thought he was ill and gave some of his work to his colleague Janice.
....
....
12. So when he finally got to work late, the boss gave him a new project, working with a firm of architects.
....
....
13. He was surprised to find out that the receptionist at the architects' was an old school friend that he hadn't seen for years; he was delighted that the boss hadn't given the job to someone else.
....
....
14. The boss said she had meant to give the project to Janice, but gave it to Chris because Janice had already started on his old project.
....
....

2 Put one of the words or expressions from the box into each blank.

bite chips chips escaped felt sorry for hurt literature physics research sausage sausage shared stand well off wild working class

I was thinking the other day about my university days, when I .... a flat with a girl named Ruth Benson. I was studying .... and hoping to become a .... scientist; while Ruth was studying English .... She didn't have a very clear idea of what she wanted to do then; she used to say that it was a bit of a surprise for a .... girl whose father was a coal miner to go to university at all. (She later started writing novels, and good ones; she's quite .... now, in fact.)

Anyway, I was thinking about the time we shared our lunch with a monkey. We were both studying one afternoon when this funny little monkey with big eyes and a white beard came through the window. I didn't want to get near it at first; it looked frightened and I was afraid it would .... me. But Ruth talked to it and offered it some .... and .... (the remains of our lunch, bought at a .... across the street from the flat). It loved the .... but wouldn't touch the ....; the food seemed to calm it down a bit. It didn't seem ...., so we thought it was a pet. It was very interested in exploring our room. When it started moving around we saw that its leg was .... We both .... it, but weren't quite sure what to do. We decided that Ruth should stay in the flat with it while I went to phone a vet. The vet put a bandage on the leg and helped us find the owners – the monkey had .... from a small local zoo. Neither Ruth nor I had done much studying that afternoon, but we had an original excuse to give to our tutors the next day.

3 Pronunciation. Say these sentences with the right stress.

1. If she'd been **bad** at **lang**uages, she would have **stu**died **maths**.
2. She'd have be**come** a **tea**cher if she'd **stu**died **maths**.
3. If her **pa**rents had been **work**ing **class**, she'd have **gone** to **teach**er **train**ing **col**lege.
4. If she'd **gone** to **teach**er **train**ing **col**lege, she would have **met** Alice **there**.
5. She **would**n't have **met** **An**drew if her **pa**rents had been **work**ing **class**.
6. If she **had**n't **met** **An**drew, she **would**n't have **gone** to **Crete**.

4 Revision. Choose the right verb form for each sentence.

'Hello? Oh, hello. Can you hold on a minute? – Neil *drinks / is drinking* the cat's milk. (. . .) Hello again. Yes, I did ring earlier. You know we usually *go / are going* to see my family for the Christmas holidays. (. . .) Yeah. Well, mother *works / 's working* in Cleveland right now, and she won't be home until early in January. My brother invited us to come and have Christmas dinner with them – you know they *have / are having* a big house by the sea. But we've decided to have a complete change instead: we *go / are going* to Florida! (. . .) Yes, isn't it exciting? Well, the thing is, we wondered if you could look after Andy's hamsters while we're gone? (. . .) Yes, that's right. You've seen the cage; it's not too big. They *just eat / are just eating* a few sunflower seeds and a bit of carrot or lettuce; they're not much trouble, really. (. . .) Would you? That's really kind, Jack, I promise I'll bring you back a nice present. (. . .) Well, the flight is very early on the morning of the 18th, but we *spend / are spending* the night in a hotel near the airport, so could I bring them over on the 17th? (. . .) After five. Sure. Listen, thanks a lot, Jack. Oh God! I've got to go. Neil *tries / is trying* to play one of his dad's records. See you, Jack. Thanks a lot.'

5 Read Exercise 3 in Practice Book Lesson 27A again. Then write ten or more sentences about how you think children today are different from when you or your parents were children. Say which of the changes you think are good and which are bad.

6 Try the crossword.

ACROSS

1. A group of people who meet to make laws.
5. I don't like it as much as they . . . .
6. . . . dear! My passport is gone!
7. Is Brazil in South America?
9. I usually . . . up my desk before I leave work.
10. Am, are, ...
11. Our company has a new managing ....
14. The police .... an extremist political group of planting the bomb.
16. You buy stamps at a .... office.
18. Opposite of *from*.
19. I was late, ... I decided to drive.
21. Cut with teeth.
22. A part of the body between neck and waist.
23. A word like *a*.
24. Your brakes won't .... out so quickly if you use your gears to slow down.
26. Large swimming mammals.
28. Were both your parents English?
30. After childhood.
33. I don't get .... with my sister very well.
34. Some people think he made the world.
35. 'Have you finished paying for your car?' 'No, I still .... £500 or so on it.'
36. Past of *is*.
37. Opposite of *out*.

DOWN

1. Study of the laws of the universe.
2. Who is .... for this mistake?
3. I always suspect the party that has a .... in Parliament
4. The Pope is .... Chinese.
5. Opposite of *wet*.
8. If I .... known, I would have told you.
12. Last year we had a .... winter – cold and rainy – but this year it has been surprisingly warm.
13. Iron, water and air make this happen.
15. You will die if you don't.
17. Not city, not village.
19. Usually made of pork.
20. Is the heating ....?
24. Paper is made of this.
25. What a car does if you leave it outside long enough.
26. Seven days.
27. There is always some of this at the top of high mountains.
29. 'Could you hand me those trousers, please?' 'Which ....?'
31. I don't know if I can help you, but I'll .... what I can.
32. How high .... you jump?
35. I looked out .... the window.

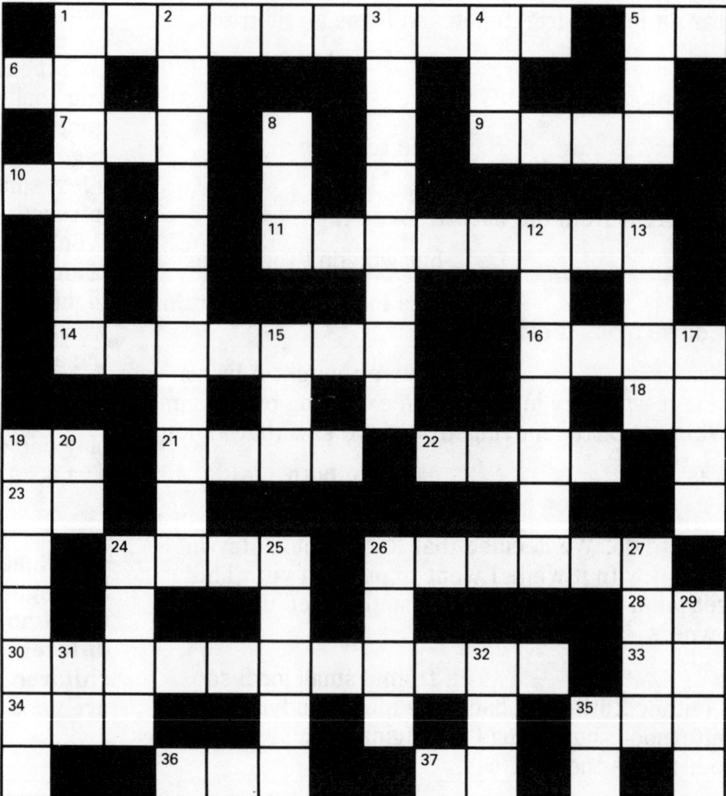

(Solution on page 144.)

Health

A Taking regular exercise

1 Put the correct form of the verb in each sentence.

1. ...Running... when you have got a cold is bad for your health. (*run*)
2. I'd like .... more regular exercise than I do. (*take*)
3. I like .... tennis, but I can't really get excited about .... (*play*; *run*)
4. .... is actually very good exercise if you do it regularly. (*dance*)
5. I'm not really tall enough .... basketball. (*play*)
6. My doctor has told me not .... so much alcohol. (*drink*)
7. We try .... good quality food at home, but I think the children eat a lot of junk when they're out. (*eat*)
8. I think .... can be bad for you if it means that your weight is always going up and down a lot. (*diet*)

2 Complete these sentences any way you like.

1. I like women who ....
2. I like men who ....
3. I like films that ....
4. I like the sort of music my mother ....
5. When I was small, I went to a school that ....
6. The friends I ....
7. My boss/teacher is a person who ....

3 Put each sentence in order.

1. Christmas we about brother book gave for my a exercise . ...

....

2. sister me my theatre promised evening the at an . ...

....

3. lend could pen me minute you for your a ? ....

....

4. always story read Timmy a I bedtime at . ...

....

5. pounds five me owes Geoff . ...

....

6. invitation the Allcocks send you an did ? ....

....

4 Fill the blanks with words from the box.

avoid breathe cause chemicals example exercise headaches health healthier regularly share smoke

I do my best to take care of my ...., and my family's, but it's not always easy. My wife and I .... the cooking and shopping, and I'm a bit more careful than she is about buying foods that don't have colourings or other sorts of .... in. I know you can't .... things like that entirely, but I really try to do my best. I think that chemicals probably .... more health problems than most people think they do.

We don't ...., and in fact don't have many friends who do; but my mother can't live without her cigarettes, and of course when she is here all of the air we .... has some smoke in it.

The whole family gets some kind of ....: both the kids are very keen swimmers, my wife runs .... and I play squash at least three times a week.

Actually I think we are .... now than when we were younger; we began paying more attention to food when the kids were young, and wanted to give them a good .... by keeping fit ourselves. I certainly get fewer ...., colds and flu than I did then.

5 Grammar revision. Put in *a/an* or *the* where necessary.

1. I often go to ....–.... bed late.
2. Have you ever had ...an... operation?
3. .... medical care is free in Fantasia.
4. Do you often have .... headaches?
5. My brother's .... dentist.
6. I don't get ill very often – perhaps once .... year.
7. .... National Health Service was set up in Britain in 1946.
8. In many countries you have to pay for .... medical treatment.
9. If a person goes to a doctor, ... doctor may give .... person .... prescription for some medicine.
10. The patient takes .... prescription to .... pharmacist.
11. .... people in Britain have to pay part of .... cost of their glasses.

6 How many words do you know for the parts of a car? Label as many parts as you can.

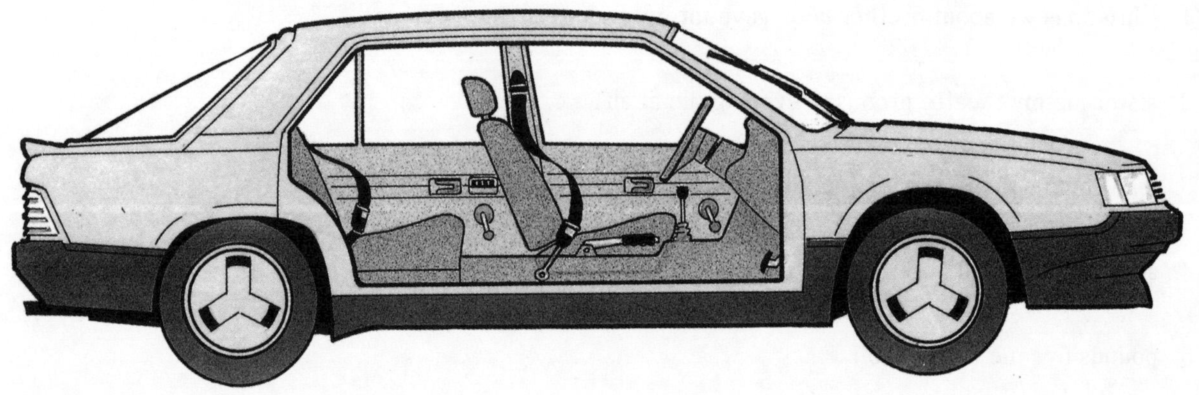

7 **Read this without a dictionary. Mark the words whose meanings you can guess like (this.) Are there any words that you have to look up in order to understand the text? If there are, mark them like <u>this</u> and look them up before reading the text again. Then look on page 144.**

THE TWENTIETH CENTURY DISEASE: FOOD ALLERGY

I met Julie at a friend's house. Among the people gathered round the table for dinner, she was the odd one out. She scarcely talked. When she did talk, she didn't smile. And after supper, when everyone else was involved in conversation, she sat with a book in the corner.

Just one week later, Julie rang me up. I didn't recognise the voice which came bubbling over the wire, it was so cheerful and alive. 'I can't believe it,' she said. 'I feel like a new person. I haven't felt so well for years!'

Julie had turned out to be one of the millions who, without knowing it, are allergic to everyday foods and chemicals. The results can be serious. An extreme case, which was reported recently, is that of former pop-singer Sheila Rossall, who is threatened by contact with almost every product of twentieth-century life; she cannot even use a telephone because she reacts to the plastic it is made from. Sheila's case is extreme. But there are also millions of people like Julie, who are not ill, but who are not well either. 'In a typical doctor's surgery, about one third of the patients are suffering from allergic symptoms,' says Dr Richard Mackarness, 'and another third have their problems worsened by allergy. Many of these people will end up being told that their problems are "psychosomatic" – in the mind. But they're not – they're caused by such everyday things as the food they eat or the air they breathe.'

Headaches, depression, tiredness, high blood pressure, stomach ulcers are just some of the conditions which can be caused by unrecognised allergies. Often avoiding a few things can improve a person's health greatly. When Julie stopped eating wheat and cheese and drinking coffee, her whole life changed.

But many doctors do not have the time or the training to recognise allergies. If you think you may have an allergy problem, the best approach is to read one of the books listed below and to ask for the help of one of the groups whose addresses are given.

(from an article by Jane Firbank in *Cosmopolitan* – adapted)

Where does it hurt?

1 **Put one of the words or expressions from the box into each sentence. You can usually choose from several words or expressions for each sentence; but you must put the one you choose into the right place in the sentence! Examples:**

My back ^*never* hurts. **OR** My back hurts ^*all the time*.

always ever never often sometimes
usually all the time every year
three or four times a week when it's cold

1. I can't walk upstairs without a lot of pain.
2. I get very tired after I eat.
3. My neck hurts.
4. I get headaches in the spring.
5. Is the pain very bad?
6. Does it hurt when you talk?
7. It's very painful.
8. I feel sort of funny.
9. Does your leg itch?
10. I have terrible indigestion.

2 **Write about the following situations without using quotation marks ('...'). Use the correct forms of *ask, tell* and *advise.***

1. David said to Eric, 'Get out of my house!'
   David told Eric to get out of his house.
2. The man next to me smiled and said, 'I wonder if you'd mind watching my dog for a minute?'
   The man next to me smiled and asked me to watch his dog for a minute.
3. Jane's daughter said, 'Could I borrow your blue sweater?'
   Jane's daughter asked if she could borrow my blue sweater.
4. 'You should ask for more information,' I told Joanne.
   I advised Joanne to ask for more information.
5. 'Just breathe in and out through your mouth now,' the doctor told Alan.
6. 'I really think you'd better see a specialist,' the doctor said to Anne. (Use *advise.*)
7. My mother rang up and said, 'Could you possibly come a bit earlier?'
8. 'Can you lend me five pounds till Monday?' Gerry asked Claire.
9. 'Don't tell anyone else,' the big man said to his friend.
10. 'You should ask for a second opinion,' the lawyer told Tom.
11. 'Do have a drink,' Fiona told us.
12. The man looked up shyly and said to me, 'Would you mind if I smoked?'

3 Fill in the conversation with words and expressions from the box.

a about ago all the time bad chest did exactly have hurts just here pain problem see smoke to to breathe whole working worse

D: Good morning, Mr Harris. What's the ....?

P: Well, I've got a very bad .... in my ...., doctor.

D: I .... How long .... you had it? When .... it start?

P: .... a week ....

D: Do you have the pain ....?

P: Well, it's .... when I get up in the morning. But it's there the .... time, yes. Sometimes it's so .... it stops me ....

D: Is it bad now?

P: Not too good. It really ....

D: Do you ....?

P: Occasionally. One or two .... day.

D: Now where .... is the pain?

P: ....

D: All right. Now I want you .... in and out slowly, and I'll listen .... your chest.

4 Write the patient's side of the conversation.

D: Good morning. Please sit down. Now, what's the problem?

P: ....

D: I see. When did it start?

P: ....

D: Does it hurt all the time?

P: ....

D: Where exactly does it hurt?

P: ....

D: And have you had this problem before?

P: ....

D: Have you had other illnesses in the last year or so?

P: ....

D: All right. Now I'm going to examine you. I'd like you to take your clothes off and lie down over there, please.

5 Revision. Put in the correct prepositions.

1. I'll see you .... five o'clock.
2. The next meeting's .... Tuesday morning.
3. Are you going away .... Christmas?
4. We met them when we were .... holiday.
5. They live .... Walton Street.
6. Who do you want to talk ....?
7. 'Which is your house?' 'The one .... the green door.'
8. You're not listening .... me.
9. They're always talking .... the same thing.
10. Did you pay .... the drinks?
11. That's very kind .... you.
12. I think he's too old .... her.
13. Local authorities are responsible .... education.
14. There are big differences .... the British and American systems.
15. Animals can be divided .... several different families.
16. Some birds are unable to fly – .... instance, penguins.

6 Write about a time when you were in hospital or ill (or you can write about someone you know).

Heads

A What sort of brain have you got?

1 Put in words from the box.

common sense deal with decisions facts forget imagination logical memory planning remember

1. I've got a terrible .... for names, but I can usually .... faces.
2. People sometimes say that men are more .... than women, but I don't think it's true.
3. Army officers need to be good at making ....
4. I think we should start .... our holiday soon.
5. That child's got an extraordinary .... He's always making up stories.
6. I shall never .... meeting my wife for the first time.
7. He's very intelligent, but I don't think he's got much ....
8. A historian needs to be able to .... large numbers of ....

2 Put in *always, never, sometimes, often, occasionally, quite often* or *hardly ever.*

1. Most people forget names.
   ....
2. I go dancing.
   ....
3. I wash my own clothes.
   ....
4. I speak English.
   ....
5. It rains in August in my country.
   ....
6. I forget faces.
   ....
7. I smoke.
   ....
8. I drink whisky.
   ....
9. I fall in love.
   ....
10. I travel by air.
   ....

3 Put in *when* or *if.*

1. .... he dies, his money will all go to charity.
2. I'll telephone you this evening .... I have time.
3. She was beautiful .... she was young.
4. It's a nice place to live .... you like a quiet life.
5. .... there's another war, we'll all be killed.
6. What will you do .... you can't find a job next year?
7. Don't forget to put the lights out .... you go to bed.
8. He'll be a very good-looking boy .... he's older, I think.

4 Put in the right verb form.

1. I'll tell you as soon as I .... (*know*)
2. If I .... George, I'll tell him to come and see you. (*see*)
3. I .... happy when this job is finished. (*be*)
4. What .... if the police find out? (*happen*)
5. What will you do if you .... find your keys? (*cannot*)
6. My father says he'll give me the money for my studies if I .... it. (*need*)
7. It'll be nice when we .... back home again. (*be*)
8. When it stops raining, I think I .... some gardening. (*do*)

"Of course I remember you're my ex-wife – it's your name that escapes me!"

5 **Read one or both of these texts with a dictionary.**

A BOY'S HEAD

In it there is a space-ship
and a project
for doing away with piano lessons.

And there is
Noah's ark,
which shall be first.

And there is
an entirely new bird,
an entirely new hare,
an entirely new bumble-bee.

There is a river
that flows upwards

There is a multiplication table.

There is anti-matter.

And it just cannot be trimmed.

I believe
that only what cannot be trimmed
is a head.

There is much promise
in the circumstance
that so many people have heads.

(Miroslav Holub, translated by Ian Milner)

My thoughts

I sometimes wonder what my mind is like inside, often I fancy that it is like this. I feel as if my mind goes round and round like the earth and if my lessons make me think hard it begins to spin. In my other class it was getting all stodgy and still and lumpy and rusty. I feel as if there is a ball in my mind and it is divided into pieces – each piece stands for a different mood. The ball turns every now and then and that's what makes me change moods. I have my learning mood, my goodlooks mood, my happy mood, my loose-end mood and my grumpy mood, my missrable mood, my thoughtful mood and my planning mood. At the moment I am writing this I am in my thoughtful mood. When I am in my thoughtful mood I think out my maths and plan stories and poems. When my kitten is in her thoughtful mood she thinks shall I pounce or not, and shall I go to sleep or not. This sort of thing goes on in my own mind too. It is very hard for me to put my thoughts into words.

Sarah Gristwood, aged 7

Take your choice

1 **How quick-thinking are you? How accurate are you?**
First, read right through all the sentences.
Then do what they tell you as fast as you can.
Time limit: 90 seconds.

1. Write your name.
2. Double your age and write the result.
3. Write the name of your country backwards.
4. Draw a big square.
5. Put a small circle in the square.
6. If it is Tuesday, write 'X'; if not, write the letter before X in the English alphabet.
7. Write the name of the day before the day before yesterday.
8. If your birthday is in the first half of the month, write the name of the month; if not, write the year of your birth.
9. Don't write the name of the British Prime Minister.
10. Only answer the first question.

2 **Vocabulary revision.**

Your grandfather is your mother's father or your father's father.
Your aunt is your mother's sister, or your father's sister, or your mother's or father's brother's wife.
What are: your uncle; your grandmother; your cousin; your niece; your nephew; your great-grandfather?
What is your mother's sister's husband's wife's mother?

3 **Look at the statistics and make five sentences. Examples:**

209,000 houses a year were built from 1945 to 1955.
More houses were built in 1979 than in 1980.

Houses and flats completed: annual averages and actuals, United Kingdom — thousands

	Total	Local authorities and New Towns	Other public sector	Private owners
1945-55[1]	209·0	154·8	8·5	45·6
1956-65[1]	317·9	142·5	6·9	168·5
1965-75[1]	357·9	157·2	11·9	188·7
1976	324·8	151·8	17·7	155·2
1977	313·5	143·3	26·9	143·3
1978	288·1	112·4	24·0	151·7
1979	241·9	85·7	19·0	137·2
1980	238·9	88·3	21·3	129·3
Totals completed 1945-1979				
England and Wales	8896·8	4227·1	340·5	4329·1
Scotland	1053·5	798·5	24·4	230·6
Northern Ireland	275·2	172·4	1·4	101·5
	10225·5	5198·0	366·3	4661·2

[1]Annual average

(from *Guinness Book of Facts*)

4 **Read this text with a dictionary.**

QUICK-THINKING VAN DRIVER

A quick-thinking van driver rescued 11 people trapped in a blazing house in Birkenhead early today.

Mr Cliff Stanton of Halwood was driving past a house in Beaufort Road when he saw the ground floor ablaze. Four adults and seven children were trapped in the bedroom above.

Mr Stanton smartly backed his van across the pavement, smashed through the front fence, and drove up to the front of the house. The trapped occupants were able to scramble to safety via the van's roof.

(News report, 16 May 1983)

5 **Write about a time when you (or somebody you know) got out of trouble by thinking quickly.**

Work

A Working makes me think

1 Choose the infinitive or the *-ing* form.

1. I want *to change* / *changing* my job.
2. Do you enjoy *to travel* / *travelling*?
3. Would you like *to be* / *being* a commercial traveller?
4. When I'm with you I can't stop *to laugh* / *laughing*.
5. I hate *to watch* / *watching* tennis.
6. I'm not very interested in *discuss* / *discussing* your problems.
7. I remember *to meet* / *meeting* you about five years ago.
8. Should I *come* / *coming* to work early tomorrow?
9. *To have* / *Having* a lot of freedom is very important to me.
10. Thomas Edison was well known for *to work* / *working* very long hours.

2 Can you find all these things in the picture?

computer terminal desk file
filing cabinet lamp photocopier
shelves telephone directory
telephone switchboard typewriter
waste-paper bin

3 Read this text once without a dictionary.
If you find a word whose meaning you cannot guess, underline it like this. If you think you can guess what a new word means, circle it and write your definition or translation in the margin, like this: margin
Then look up the words in the dictionary, check your guesses, and read the text again.

empty space at side of text

'It was all his own idea,' says Pat Peters, the 38-year-old wife of Palo Alto, California high school football coach Bob Peters, 39. Bob had just drawn up a 'motherhood contract' – a document stating that for 70 days this summer he would take over the care and feeding of the couple's four children, plus all household chores. Although he didn't even know how to make coffee when he signed, he was supremely confident. (He thought the experience would make a cute book.)

After 40 of the 70 days, he was ready to give up. 'I was beaten down, completely humbled,' admits Peters. Three weeks later he spoke to the local press (also part of the bargain), stating, 'Not only is motherhood a difficult task, not only is it never-ending, it is an impossible job for any normal human being.'

Bob and Pat were high school sweethearts. After they were married in 1960, she worked as a secretary to help put him through university. Since then Bob has been the football and wrestling coach at Palo Alto's Cubberley High while Pat raised the kids.

Then two years ago Pat went back to work as a secretary at Cubberley. 'I had been around children so much,' she sighs, 'I couldn't talk to a grown-up.' She continued to run the household, however – until Bob signed the contract, whereupon she decided to relax and enjoy it.

Although Peters had consulted with his school's home economics teachers and the head of the cafeteria, his meals were sometimes a disaster. 'I tried to slip the butter I'd forgotten under the eggs after they were frying,' he says. For the last three weeks, the family ate out a lot – sometimes having Macdonald's hamburgers for lunch *and* dinner.

As for housekeeping, a home economics teacher had told Bob that a room always looks clean if the bed is made. 'I found an easier way – I shut the doors,' he says. Soon the kids were wearing the same clothes for a week. 'I made them wear their shirts inside out, and when we went to pick up Pat at work they turned them right side out so they would look clean.'

Now that Bob has publicly admitted he was wrong, he is routinely sharing the child-raising and household tasks with Pat. The tentative title of his book about the summer is taken from something he shouted at the kids one day: 'Wait till your mother gets home!'

(from an article by Nancy Faber in *People Weekly* – adapted)

4 Put an expression from the box into each blank. You will not use all the words.

someone else	anyone else	everyone else	somewhere else	anywhere else
everywhere else	something else	anything else	everything else	who else
where else	what else	how else	why else	

1. I'm going to the shop to get some cheese – do we need ....?
2. I can't go to the meeting tomorrow; .... will have to go.
3. The burglar must have had a key – .... could he have got in?
4. George was late, as usual, but .... was on time.
5. I had .... to tell you, but I can't remember what it was.
6. .... is coming besides Margaret and Ian?
7. I'll buy some crisps and peanuts for the party – .... do you think I should get?
8. I was always .... when Janice came to the office, so I never spoke to her, except on the phone.
9. Is .... going with you tonight, or are you going alone?
10. If you carry that box, I think I can get ....

5 Revision. Fill in the table of irregular verbs. Learn the ones you don't know.

PRESENT	PAST TENSE	PAST PARTICIPLE
break	broke	broken
build	....	....
grow	....	....
hide	....	....
keep	....	....
let	....	....
lose	....	....
stick	....	....
take	....	....
wear	....	....
wind	....	....

B Do you have to work long hours?

1 **What do you have to do when you work? Write down as many things as possible.**

2 **Read the story (use your dictionary if you need to), and then write what you think Gwyneth should do and why. Write eight or more sentences.**

Gwyneth Jones teaches mathematics at a university. She has a secure job, enjoys her teaching and research, and gets on well with her supervisor and her colleagues.

Some ex-classmates of Gwyneth's have offered her the chance to join them in a new company to produce computer software for businesses. They have had no trouble getting loans from the bank to start the business, and everyone thinks that it will do very well. Of course, the amount of money the partners earn will depend on how well the business does; but Gwyneth will probably earn a lot more money than she does at the university.

What do you think Gwyneth should do? The new company is very exciting, and the money might be very good indeed. On the other hand, she is happy teaching and doing research. Oh, yes – she's going to have a baby in a few months' time, but she has always planned to continue working after the child is born.

....

....

....

....

....

....

....

3 **Revision. Put the correct form of the verb in each sentence.**

1. Gunpowder ....was invented..... by the Chinese several centuries ago. (*invent*)
2. No woman .... ever .... President of the United States. (*elected*)
3. I .... about losing my job, but I don't worry about it now. (*frighten*)
4. Ruth is disappointed; the job she applied for .... to someone with more experience. (*give*)
5. Before the Princess arrived at the shipyard, police dogs .... to make sure there were no bombs hidden there. (*use*)
6. When .... the new shop .... – this year or next? (*open*)
7. Most of the businesses in our town .... by local people now. (*own*)
8. Aren't you afraid you .... if you don't start coming to work on time? (*sack*)

4 **Revision. /ɪ/ or /ə/? Underline the stressed syllable in each word. Then draw a square around the first vowel in the work if it is pronounced /ɪ/; and a circle around the first vowel if it is pronounced /ə/. Look back at Student's Book 27B if you have problems.**

machine improve collect predict essential

discover together announce adopt belief

instructions Olympic

5 Try the crossword.

ACROSS

4. Some people like to listen to music when they read, but I can't .... with music playing.
7. Opposite of *off*.
8. What's she taking out .... her handbag?
10. She goes to the same hairdresser as I ....
11. How to get some liquid out of a bottle.
12. I feel very funny. I think I'd better .... down.
13. Tell someone what you think they should do.
14. I don't use that washing-up liquid any more – it made my hands ....
18. Opposite of *far*.
20. A technician, a draughtswoman, ... engineer.
21. You might take this if you are ill.
22. You can sometimes see this in the sky at night.
24. What you get for working.

DOWN

1. Past of *win*.
2. The first step in solving a problem is to .... it.
3. One of these is not enough to stand on.
4. Opposite of *make simpler*.
5. There are more people in this building on a Sunday than on any other day.
6. Opposite of *look for*.
9. Hay ....
10. He comes to your house for rubbish.
12. Opposite of *early*.
15. Something to tidy your hair with.
17. Don't throw away.
19. An organisation of men and a few women; most of them have guns.
23. On top .... the television.

(Solution on page 144.)

Travel

A Where are they?

1 **You can go to a travel agent's to make enquiries about a holiday, to buy an air ticket to New York, because you want to make a reservation on a train, and for lots of other reasons.**
You can go to a petrol station to buy petrol, to have the oil checked, because the petrol pump attendant is a friend of yours, etc.
Why did you last go to:
a petrol station; a travel agent's; an airport; a bus stop; a garage; a station enquiry office; a police station; a post office; a bank?
(Answer with *To . . .* or *Because . . .*)

....

....

....

....

....

....

....

....

....

....

....

....

2 **Put in the right question-tags.**

1. It's a nice day, isn't it? ....
2. You look very like your father, ...
3. You aren't tired, ...
4. Mary doesn't drink wine, ...
5. Your mother speaks Chinese, ...
6. The garden's looking nice, ...
7. People are all different, ...
8. You've got a cold, ...
9. He doesn't drive very well, ...
10. You want to speak to the manager, ...

3 **Vocabulary revision. Which word is different? (Answers on page 144.)**

1. analyse buy classify think plan
2. explain ask tell think suggest
3. older worse better more important easy
4. on in before at in front of top
5. day journey minute hour second
6. friend lorry driver architect teacher doctor
7. driver painter hospital plumber waiter
8. postal order stamp telegram newspaper

4 **Put in *anybody, somebody, nobody, everybody, anything, something, nothing* or *everything.***

1. I think there's .... at the door.
2. I'm sorry – I haven't got .... for you to drink.
3. I think you know .... who's here, don't you?
4. ....'s worrying me – can I talk to you about it?
5. .... really knows what goes on inside children's heads.
6. Has .... seen Janet today?
7. She had her bag stolen in London: she lost her passport, her money, her air ticket – ....
8. 'Would you like a sandwich?' 'No, ... to eat, thank you.'

5 **Imagine you are standing outside the main post office in a city or town in your country. Somebody asks you the way to a bank, or a railway station, or a museum, or somewhere else (you decide exactly where). Write what you will say to him or her.**

6 Read this with a dictionary.

The scientist Thomas Young could read when he was two years old, and had read the Bible twice when he was four. He learnt 12 languages as a child, and could play a large number of musical instruments.

By the age of 13, the French linguist Champollion had learnt Latin, Greek, Hebrew, Arabic, Syrian, Chaldean and Coptic. When he was 21, he solved the mystery of ancient Egyptian hieroglyphic writing.

Sir John Bowring (1792–1872) was said to be able to read 200 languages and speak 100. The New Zealander Dr Harold Whitmore Williams could communicate in 52 languages, and was fluent in 28.

Five hundred years ago Leonardo da Vinci produced designs for a parachute, a life jacket, a water pump, a paddle boat, a steam gun, a lens-grinding machine, a machine gun, a helicopter, a submarine, and a number of other modern inventions. He was also one of the greatest artists that have ever lived.

The American chess master Morphy once played eight games of chess simultaneously while blindfolded. (He won six of the games.)

The most intelligent living person may be the Korean Kim Ung-Yong, born in 1963. At the age of four he could speak Korean, Japanese, English and German, had published poetry, and could solve problems in integral calculus.

Who has the right of way . . . ?

1 Put in the right prepositions. (Sometimes more than one might be possible.)

at	behind	by	in	in front of	near
on	out of	under			

1. I met my wife .... a dance.
2. We live very .... John and Peter.
3. I wish he wouldn't drive so close .... us – if we have to stop suddenly he'll run into us.
4. Don't throw bottles .... the window, please.
5. 'Where's my supper?' '........................ the oven.'
6. Can I sit .... you?
7. Whenever I get a good seat at the cinema, somebody tall always comes and sits .... me.
8. We're travelling .... the ten o'clock train.
9. Have you looked .... the bed? It's really dirty.

2 Why do the British drive on the left? Read this with a dictionary and find out.

1. The heart is on the left side of the body.

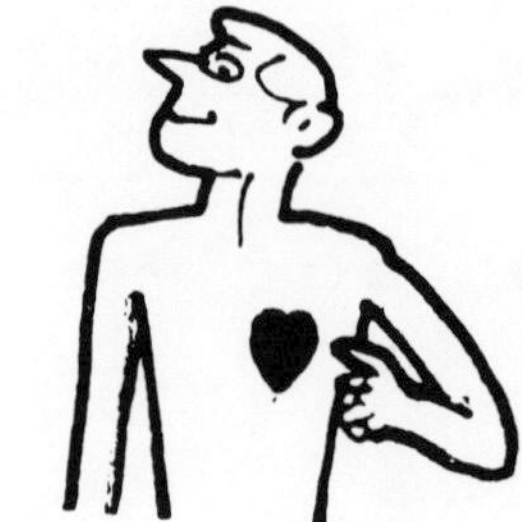

2. Hundreds of years ago, soldiers fought with swords.

3. They used shields to protect their hearts. The shields were naturally held in the left hand.

4. The sword was therefore held in the right hand.

5. It was therefore natural to put the sword away on the left side of the body.

6. If you have a sword hanging down on the left, which side do you get on a horse from? Not from the horse's right.

7. You get on from the horse's left.

8. If you are getting on to a horse from its left, which side of the road do you stand on? Not on the right.

9. You stand on the left-hand side of the road, get on the horse in comfort, and ride away on the left? It's logical.

10. Now can you explain why foreigners drive on the right?

3 **Can you sort these words into two groups, according to the pronunciation of *th*?**

think with bath mother then three together both although thank thing through clothes these

4 **Look at the picture. What do you think is going to happen? Why?**

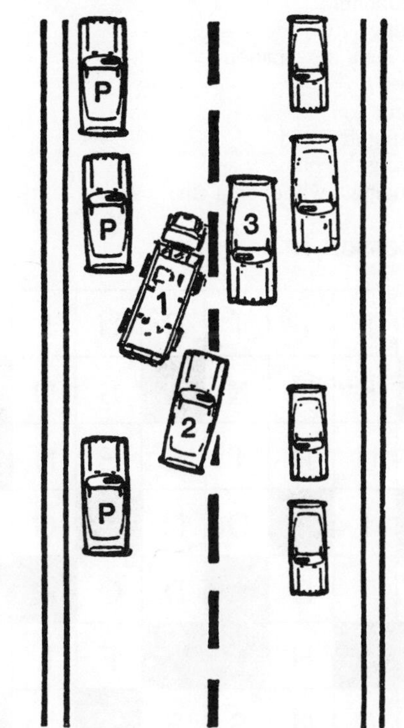

A very common type of accident. Cars marked "P" are parked.
(from *Car Driving in Two Weeks*)

5 **Write about the traffic regulations in your country.**
OR: Write the story of an accident.

Answers to Exercises

Unit 2, Lesson A

3 The woman is:

A. drinking a glass of wine
B. having a bath
C. telephoning
D. driving
E. reading a newspaper
F. cooking
G. typing
H. getting dressed
I. playing the piano
J. changing a wheel on a car.

Unit 3, Lesson B

1 D	I	2 F	3 F	4 I	C	5 U	6 L	T
I		7 R	U	N		8 S	O	
9 F	O	U	R	T	10 E	E	N	
F		I		11 O	N		12 G	O
13 E	A	T	14 S		15 D	16 O		
R			H			17 F	18 L	Y
19 E	X	C	U	20 S	21 E		I	
N			22 T	H	A	N	K	S
T		23 U	S	E	R		E	

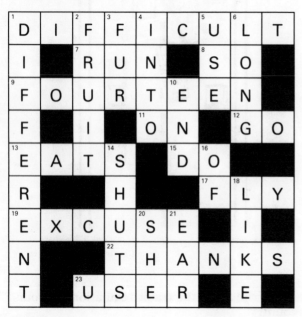

Unit 4, Lesson A

5 In picture B:

The man has longer hair; he is taller and thinner.
The woman is a bit fatter; she has bigger feet, shorter hair and a shorter skirt.
The picture on the wall is higher.
The room door is wider.
There are two cushions on the sofa.
The cat is smaller.

Unit 6, Lesson B

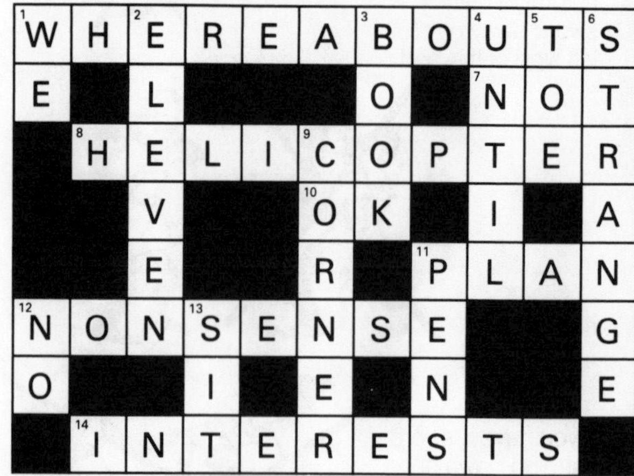

1 W	H	2 E	R	E	A	3 B	O	4 U	5 T	6 S
E		L				O		7 N	O	T
	8 H	E	L	I	9 C	O	P	T	E	R
		V			10 O	K		I		A
		E			R		11 P	L	A	N
12 N	O	N	13 S	E	N	S	E			G
O			I		E		N			E
	14 I	N	T	E	R	E	S	T	S	

Unit 7, Lesson A

5 A 1e 2b 3d 4a 5c B 1

Unit 9, Lesson A

5 4. *melon,* because it's a fruit, not a vegetable
5. *funny,* because it's abstract, not physical
6. *both,* because it's not a part of a thing
7. *tree,* because it's not a part of a plant

Unit 9, Lesson B

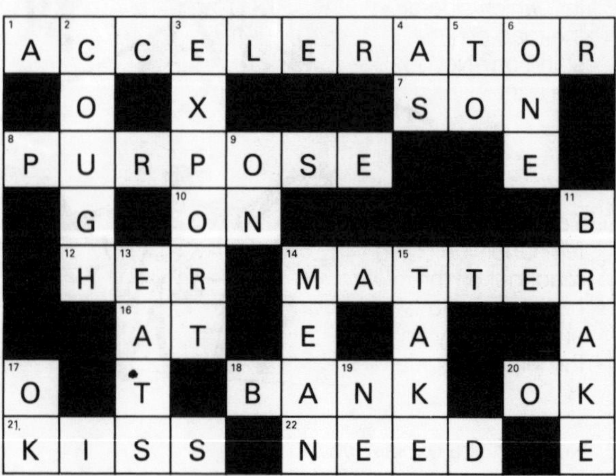

1 A	2 C	C	3 E	L	E	R	4 A	5 T	6 O	R
	O		X				7 S	O	N	
8 P	U	R	9 P	O	S	E			E	
	G		10 O	N						11 B
	12 H	13 E	R		14 M	A	15 T	T	E	R
		16 A	T		E		A			A
17 O		T		18 B	A	19 N	K		20 O	K
21 K	I	S	S		22 N	E	E	D		E

Unit 10, Lesson B

3
2. *shoe*, because it's not round
3. *fish*, because it lives in water
4. *melon*, because it's a fruit, not a vegetable
5. *funny*, because it's abstract, not physical
6. *both*, because it's not a part of a thing
7. *tree*, because it's not a part of a plant

Unit 12, Lesson B

3 James won.

8

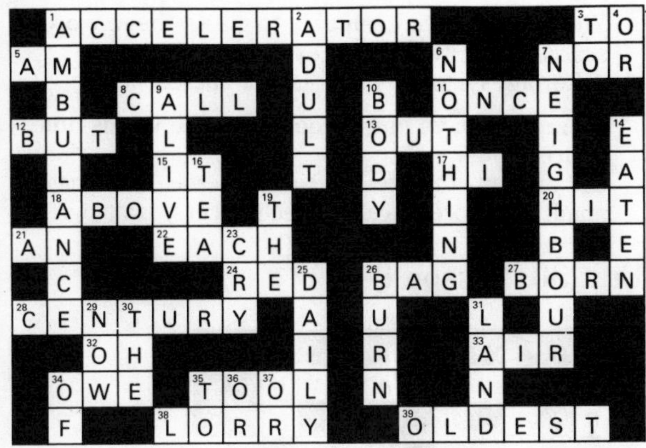

Unit 15, Lesson B

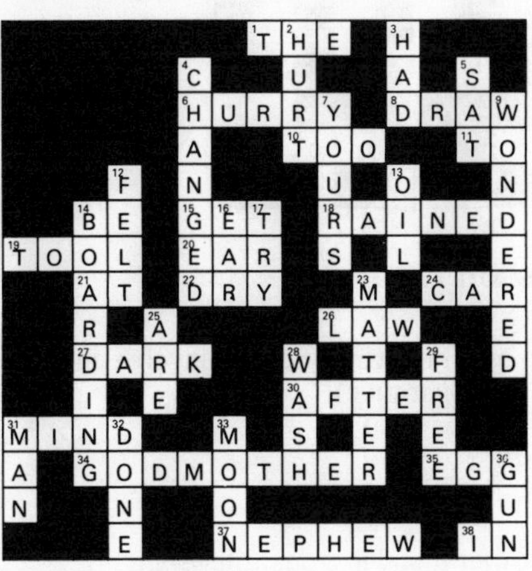

Unit 16, Lesson A

5
1. *since* (not a preposition of place)
2. *always* (the only adverb of time)
3. *east* (not personal information)
4. *pretty* (not a feeling)
5. *open* (the others are ways of speaking)
6. *book* (you don't use it to hold things)
7. *yard* (not a period of time)
8. *kiss* (not a movement)

Unit 18, Lesson B

4 1c 2c

6

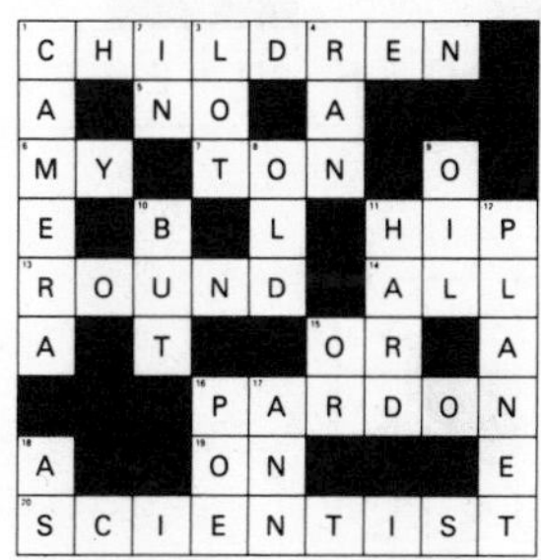

Unit 20 Lesson B

Rules for making regular past tenses and past participles:

1. **Most regular verbs:** add *-ed*.

   mend mend**ed** wait wait**ed**

2. **Verbs ending in -*e*:** add *-d*.

   manage manage**d** announce announce**d**

3. **Verbs ending in consonant + -*y*:** drop the *-y* and add *-ied*.

   empty empt**ied** hurry hurr**ied**
   worry worr**ied**
   but: play played

4. a. **Verbs ending in consonant + vowel + consonant:** double the last consonant and add *-ed*.

   rub ru**bb**ed stop sto**pp**ed
   prefer prefe**rr**ed

   b. **But: verbs like this which are not stressed at the end:** don't double the consonant; just add *-ed*.

   open open**ed** order order**ed**

   c. **And: never double final *w*, *x* or *y*.**

   slow slowed mix mixed
   play played

Unit 21, Lesson B

T	U	R	N	I	T	U	P			I	M
E		I		N			U		W		I
R	I	G	H	T		A	T		I	L	L
R		H		O				O	N		E
O	U	T				A	M		D		
R			D	A	N	G	E	R	O	U	S
I	N	T	O			E			W		T
S		O	N		H		N	O			A
T	A	P	E	R	E	C	O	R	D	E	R

Unit 24, Lesson B

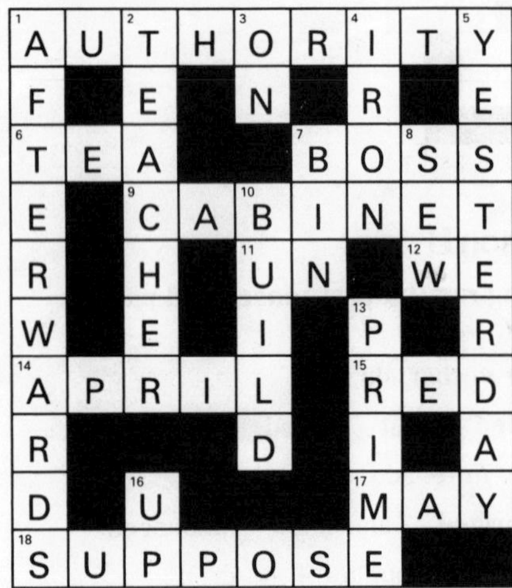

Unit 25, Lesson A

5
1. *switch* (not a piece of art)
2. *violin* (not a kind of music)
3. *eat* (not a kind of exercise)
4. *exciting* (not a feeling)
5. *worried* (not an action)
6. *chair* (not an article of clothing)
7. *Ireland* (not part of the United Kingdom)
8. *hair brush* (not a machine)
9. *bottom* (not a description of a position)

Unit 27, Lesson B

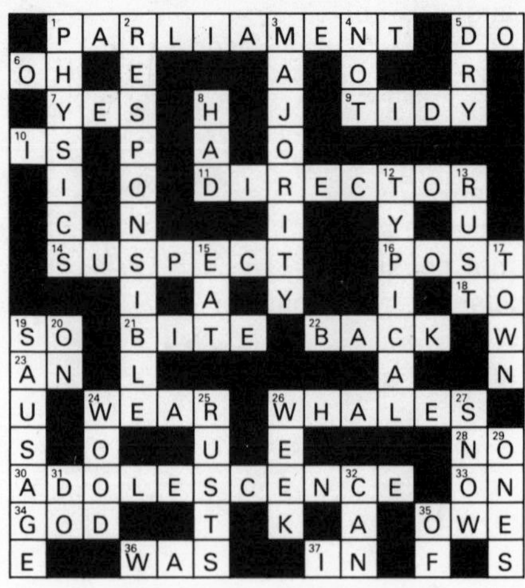

Unit 28, Lesson A

7 You should have been able to guess these words:
scarcely, involved, wire, everyday, product, suffering, symptoms, worsened, approach.

You might have had to look up these words and expressions:
odd one out, threatened, contact, case, extreme, mind, blood pressure, stomach, ulcers, training.

Unit 30, Lesson B

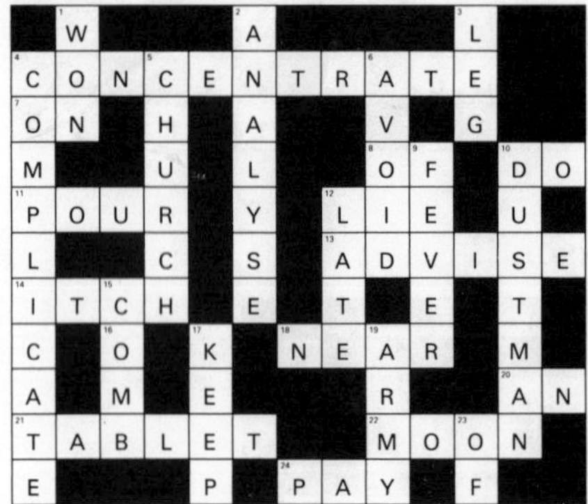

Unit 31, Lesson A

3
1. *buy*
2. *think* (the only one which doesn't involve speaking)
3. *easy* (not a comparative)
4. *top* (not a preposition)
5. *journey*
6. *friend*
7. *hospital*
8. *newspaper* (not found in a post office)